SOCIAL MYTHS AND COLLECTIVE IMAGINARIES

Myths are commonly associated with illusions or with deceptive, dangerous discourse, and are often perceived as largely the domain of premodern societies. But even in our post-industrial, technologically driven world, myths – Western or Eastern, ancient or modern, religious or scientific – are in fact powerful, pervasive forces.

In *Social Myths and Collective Imaginaries*, Gérard Bouchard conceptualizes myths as vessels of sacred values that transcend the division between primitive and modern. Myths represent key elements of collective imaginaries, past and present. In all societies there are values and beliefs that hold sway over most of the population. Whether they come from religion, political institutions, or other sources, they enjoy exalted status and go largely unchallenged. These myths have the power to bring societies together as well as pull them apart. Yet the study of myth has been largely neglected by sociologists and other social scientists. Bouchard navigates this uncharted territory by addressing a number of fundamental questions: What is the place of myth in contemporary societies and in the relations between the cultural and the social? How do myths take form? From what do they draw their strength? How do they respond to shifting contexts?

Myths matter, Bouchard argues, because of the energy they unleash, energy that enables a population to mobilize and rally around collective goals. At the same time myths work to alleviate collective anxiety and to meet the most pressing challenges facing a society. In this bold analysis, Bouchard challenges common assumptions and awakens us to the transcendent power of myth in our daily lives and in our shared aspirations.

GÉRARD BOUCHARD is a professor in the Department of Human Sciences at the Université du Québec à Chicoutimi. He is a past winner of the Governor General's Award as well as the John A. Macdonald Prize.

SOCIAL
MYTHS
and
COLLECTIVE
IMAGINARIES

Gérard Bouchard

Translated by Howard Scott

UNIVERSITY OF TORONTO PRESS
Toronto Buffalo London

© Éditions du Boréal 2015
Raison et déraison du mythe: Au coeur des imaginaires collectifs
© University of Toronto Press 2017
English-language edition
Toronto Buffalo London
www.utppublishing.com

ISBN 978-1-4426-3190-8 (cloth)
ISBN 978-1-4426-2907-3 (paper)

Library and Archives Canada Cataloguing in Publication

Bouchard, Gérard, 1943–
[Raison et déraison du mythe. English]
Social myths and collective imaginaries/Gérard Bouchard; translated by Howard Scott.–English-language edition.

Translation of: Raison et déraison du mythe.
Includes bibliographical references and index.
ISBN 978-1-4426-3190-8 (cloth).   ISBN 978-1-4426-2907-3 (paper)

1. Myth.   2. Social representation.   I. Title.   II. Title: Raison et déraison du mythe. English

BL304.B6813 2017   201'.3   C2016-906136-1

This book has been published with the help of a grant from the Canadian Federation for the Humanities and Social Sciences, through the Awards to Scholarly Publications Program, using funds provided by the Social Sciences and Humanities Research Council of Canada.

University of Toronto Press acknowledges the financial support of the Government of Canada through the National Translation Program for Book Publishing, an initiative of the *Roadmap for Canada's Official Languages 2013–2018: Education, Immigration, Communities*, for its translation activities.

University of Toronto Press acknowledges the financial assistance to its publishing program of the Canada Council for the Arts and the Ontario Arts Council, an agency of the Government of Ontario.

 Canada Council for the Arts   Conseil des Arts du Canada

 ONTARIO ARTS COUNCIL
CONSEIL DES ARTS DE L'ONTARIO
an Ontario government agency
un organisme du gouvernement de l'Ontario

Funded by the   Financé par le
Government   gouvernement
of Canada   du Canada    Canada

Contents

SOCIAL MYTHS AND COLLECTIVE IMAGINARIES

Introduction[1]

In all societies, present and past, there are values and beliefs that hold sway over most of the population. Whether they come from religion or from other forms of transcendence, they enjoy such exalted status that they go largely unchallenged. Any attempt to question them is viewed as a desecration. For example, who would attack civil liberties in England, equality of citizens in France, property rights in the United States, racial equality in South Africa, or gender equality in Quebec? These values are enveloped in emotion and have become sacred, untouchable. How did this come about?

In other words, how does a myth come into being? How does it acquire sacredness? How does it spread and reproduce? How does it go into decline? What are the roles played on the one hand by the forces of the unconscious, and on the other hand by social actors? And why don't we pay more attention to these powerful representations that express the most profound feelings of a society, that nurture identities and ideologies, that structure visions of the past and the future, and that inspire collective choices and circumscribe public debate? These questions and several others are the subject of this book.

Over the past three decades, cultural sociology has become a highly active and creative field of research, one that has taken many directions. It has generated an impressive variety of specializations, theoretical approaches, concepts, and methods. As a consequence, cultural sociology today has come to resemble a vast disorganized array of issues and avenues that defy any attempts at synthesis.[2] Yet at the same time, sociology, like all social sciences but unlike other disciplines, has strangely spurned the study of myth, this blend of imagination, emotion, reason, and sacredness that is sustained through narratives, rooted in the psyche, and used as leverage in political life.

Fundamental questions thus remain unanswered, and this one in particular: What is the place of myth in contemporary societies and in the relations between the cultural and the social? Similarly, various currents have painstakingly explored the forces that drive collective representations, especially preconscious images and mental structures. But this work is incomplete with respect to how those images or structures evolve: How do they take form? From what do they draw their strength? How do they respond to shifting contexts?[3]

These are, undeniably, very complex problems, and this book does not attempt to solve or even totally embrace them. More modestly, I will attempt to outline, within the cultural universe, one analytical approach – among many other possible ones – that is likely to address some of the deficiencies that I have just mentioned. This itinerary is centred on a specific topic – namely, social myths as representations that are key elements of collective imaginaries.

It would be reasonable to assert that this concept – the imaginary – offers access to the entire culture, as is the case with other approaches, such as structuralism, semiotics, and literary criticism. However, I will not take that direction, for various reasons, one being that the cultural sphere is too difficult to grasp in its totality. For H. J. Gans (2012), for example, the concept of culture is probably indefinable; at best, it is a notion in search of a definition (pp. 126, 131).[4] To take a convenient shortcut, I will simply say that culture refers to the more or less structured and coherent universe the symbols of which nurture the members of a collectivity[5] and govern social interactions.

I am proposing a social approach to myth as it operates in our daily lives. Such an approach, however, inevitably borrows from the main currents in cultural sociology (or the sociology of culture).[6] Generally, it follows the work of Max Weber, but also the Durkheimian tradition, which is especially concerned with the symbolic foundations of the social bond – namely, the values, beliefs, ideals, and traditions that are broadly shared in any collectivity and that underlie the sense of belonging to institutions.[7] My approach sets itself apart, however, by transposing onto current societies questions usually reserved for premodern societies and by structuring a social vision of myths and collective imaginaries.

More precisely, my approach is based on the idea that all types of myths, be they modern or premodern, proceed from a social dynamic fuelled by power strategies, divisions, conflicts, and contradictions. It also calls into question the dichotomy that has developed between the myths of so-called primitive societies and those of modern societies. In short, my endeavour is limited, focusing on a single type of collective representations, but also ambitious in that it aims to examine myths in depth and in a way that deviates at various points from the paths followed until now.[8]

This volume is constructed around five key ideas:

1 Myths are commonly associated either with illusions or with deceptive, dangerous discourse; but these are oversimplifications that prevent us from understanding the true nature of myths – a nature that goes far beyond these two familiar notions.
2 Myths remain a powerful mechanism in our societies, despite what is suggested by a still very influential tradition of thought that views them as an attribute of premodern societies and as having given way, as a result of progress, to the empire of reason.
3 The functioning of this social, symbolic mechanism, which is universal in character, has been insufficiently studied by the social sciences in recent decades.
4 There is an urgent need to examine the factors and processes that govern the birth, reproduction, and replacement of myths, which play a role today that is perhaps all the more important given that it often goes unnoticed.
5 I want to fill this gap by proposing an original model for analysing social myths, one that works at the intersection of theoretical reflection and empirical investigation.

I should point out that I give no precedence to myths and collective imaginaries over all the factors underlying social life. Nor do I claim to be clarifying the relationships or complex interactions between the cultural and the social, although I will have a few reflections to offer on this subject. Moreover, I dissociate myself from the research tradition initiated by Clifford Geertz, as well as all the structuralist theories that approach culture as if it were a coherent system. I prefer to see culture as an amalgam of (a) segments that are sometimes coherent and sometimes contradictory, but always in interaction, and (b) broad areas of indetermination.

For this reason and others, I resist the approach of Claude Lévi-Strauss to the extent that it leaves no room for emotion, which I consider a crucial component of myth. In addition, his approach is not concerned enough with researching the social roots of myth.

Finally, and somewhat shamefully, I must admit that I feel a certain discomfort with general theories. They often seem to me to establish their cohesiveness at the expense of the complexities of social life; by systematizing, they sometimes diminish or obscure as much as they clarify.

Chapter One

Myths and Collective Imaginaries

This chapter provides a rough outline of the phenomenon of myth by situating it in the universe of collective imaginaries. I will be examining the concept of myth in its various dimensions, which will make it possible to clear up a few ambiguities.

A. Myths as Sites of Superconsciousness

The question that motivates this analysis of myths can be formulated as follows. In any society or collectivity, many ideas and propositions are constantly being put forward regarding how it should be defined and governed, the values and ideals it should pursue, the role or vocation it should set for itself, the representations of the past with which it should sustain itself, the heroes it should celebrate, and so on and so forth. How do we explain why, while most of these ideas will quickly be forgotten, some will acquire an influence and authority rendering them almost sacred, so that they can impose themselves on minds and have a long-term influence on individual and collective behaviours?

In the same vein, but from another perspective, we can observe in any society key symbols and references that reveal dispositions, profound feelings, and (hyper)sensitivities. They take the form of fears, taboos, and anxieties, and rather paradoxically, they also support powerful aspirations, ideals, dominant values, beliefs, and widely accepted truths that structure visions of the world, foster identities, govern public debates, and inspire the orientations and policies of the state.

Again at the supra-individual level, these representations have a powerful influence on how a society develops, in the long term and in the short term, by providing institutions with a symbolic foundation, by bolstering ideologies and solidarity, by allowing societies to rally around specific objectives or goals, manage their tensions, and heal their divisions, and by giving them the means to rally and respond forcefully after a crisis or a traumatic event.

Together, these feelings and representations correspond to what could be called sites of *superconsciousness* – namely, the first references that lie at the core of every culture and that have a very strong hold on society given that they possess an authority akin to sacredness.[1] Belonging more to emotion than to reason, these references also permeate the minds of individuals, touch them deep inside, and motivate their choices, either by mobilizing them, by sending them forth in pursuit of bold plans, or on the contrary by inhibiting them – suffice it to contrast the reaction of Americans to the 11 September attacks of 2001, that of Haitians to the 2010 earthquake, and that of the Japanese in the wake of the Fukushima catastrophe in 2011.

Here are a few examples of these accentuated collective representations,[2] with the understanding that, from the point of view of ethics, their content can be sometimes virtuous and at other times be reprehensible (the normative load of myth, as we will see, can be negative *or* positive): racial equality in South Africa; universality and equality of rights as the foundation of citizenship in France; individual liberties in England; property rights in the United States; social equality in Norway; the mission of the workers in the ex–Soviet Union; the civilizing (and dominating) vocation of the West in the rest of the world; the superiority of the Aryan race in Nazi Germany; the desire for collective valorization in South Korea; ecological sensitivity in New Zealand (the old myth of the "garden");[3] hatred of violence and the cult of social harmony in the history of Costa Rica (C. Cruz, 2000); the attachment to the French language and the desire for national affirmation in Quebec; democracy in many of the former colonies of Europe; and gender equality throughout the West. Similarly, in many countries, people are reticent about crossing picket lines, out of respect for the workers' cause.

Over the course of its history, every society has developed this kind of attachment to values, beliefs, and ideals. It is true that over the past few decades we have observed a significant overlap, a convergence towards universal values (liberty, equality, democracy, etc.), but these still have particular flavours and vary widely in intensity from one society to another. As a legacy of events experienced over long periods of time and constantly commemorated, they are the subject of an appropriation that distinguishes them.

Once again, their hold on consciousness is such that, having been deeply internalized, they are taken for granted and surrounded by an aura that enables them in large part to avoid being questioned.[4] The symbolism of the nation provides another example. Battlefields and military cemeteries are sanctuaries (who would dare organize a party in these places?), the tomb of the unknown soldier calls for contemplation, the memory of heroes who have sacrificed their lives for the homeland is untouchable, and burning the national flag is a desecration.[5] These are mythical figures or places.

Analysis of these representations helps us understand why, during times of crisis, some societies show apathy while others demonstrate resilience and dynamism. Such analysis also helps us understand why individuals and groups are prepared to sacrifice themselves for causes even though they will never see the benefits. This being said, these primary references can also be sources of inhibition and stagnation, or they can create deep divisions, almost insoluble conflicts, collective madness, and catastrophic abuses, of which there are many examples in Western history. Finally, they can alienate a population and keep one social class or nation under the domination of another.

Readers will recognize here, at the core of culture, the heterogeneous, ambivalent, fragmented, simultaneously formidable and fascinating, and always present domain of myth.

Every community also has taboos, which are in a way the flipside of myths. These are prohibitions, institutionalized or not, accompanied by various sanctions in cases of transgression. They are manifested, for example, in a strong aversion to calling into question, or even discussing publicly, certain founding truths. But prohibitions are also unconscious desires that have never been satisfied, or they are hidden, repressed truths that would be too difficult to face – which shows that myth conceals as much as it reveals.

All of these phenomena have long been studied by philosophers, literary scholars, semiologists, and anthropologists. We can therefore base our discussion on a rich tradition of thought that clarifies many aspects of myth in various periods. This is not the place to give a detailed review of this literature – that has been done before. I will only point out that in the wake of Jung and Freud, there has been a great deal of exploration of the deep roots and symbolic structures of myth as a production of the imaginary that transcends spatio-temporal contexts (I am thinking of pioneering authors such as Gaston Bachelard, Mircea Eliade, Henri Corbin, Roger Caillois, Claude Lévi-Strauss, Northrop

Frye, and Gilbert Durand).[6] These works have mostly dealt with either the great civilizations of Antiquity or so-called archaic (or primitive) societies, and much less with modern or postmodern societies.

Given the impact and predominance of these representations in our societies, and given that they influence our lives in so many ways, one would expect to see a great deal of sociological expertise applied to the domain. Yet we know very little about the origins and development of myths, about how they are formed, perpetuated, adapted, and redefined, about the circumstances that lead them to lose their appeal and then decline, and, especially, about the process of sacralization that enables certain ideas and symbols to be transformed into sites of superconsciousness.

As fundamental as they are to understanding the world in which we live, these questions have found few answers in recent sociology. Currently, myth does not really exist as a research topic, even in cultural sociology (as A. D. Smith observed thirty years ago 1986, p. 182).[7]

This is especially the case in the United States. Focusing on structural hermeneutics, the research project "Strong Program in Cultural Sociology," proposed by J. C. Alexander and P. Smith (2001), opened up many promising horizons, but it contains only one instance of the word "myth" (in reference to the works of C. Lévi-Strauss on so-called primitive societies). The impressive anthology edited by J. C. Alexander, R. N. Jacobs, and P. Smith (2012) includes thirty chapters devoted to various themes in cultural sociology, but myths are not discussed in it; the word appears only a few times, mainly with respect to – again – the works of Lévi-Strauss and catastrophe myths. There are other important guides or textbooks in which there is practically no mention of myth – for example, those by L. Spillman (2002), R. Friedland and J. Mohr (2004), M. D. Jacobs and N. W. Hanrahan (2005), and J. R. Hall, L. Grindstaff, and M.-C. Lo (2010). The theme of myth is likewise practically absent from the works coming out of the huge international network NYLON, which includes numerous researchers in cultural sociology.[8] Paradoxically, however, the role of myths in our societies is not called into question in any of these publications.[9] Surveys of sociology literature in English Canada and Quebec have produced similar results – with one exception in Quebec, the book by H. Fisher (2004).

In Europe and elsewhere, the study of national myths is an active field, thanks especially to the pioneering work of the British sociologist Anthony D. Smith and a few periodicals devoted to the study of the nation and nationalism (e.g., *Nations and Nationalism*, *National Identities*, and *Studies in Ethnicity and Nationalism*). But the efforts at theorizing myth as a sociological mechanism have not gone very far. The emphasis has been mainly on the content, sociopolitical mapping, influence, functions, and evolution of national myths. Part of this scholarship suffers from other limitations, either because myths are associated with the premodern era, or because they are considered inconsequential fabrications, or because they are likened to tragic blunders that sometimes occur by virtue of a sort of historical inevitability.

Generally, whether in the North American or European sociological production, scholars have forgone investigating the nature and functioning of a universal mechanism that has never ceased to have profound effects on our societies, for better or for worse. Yet no society can be thought of, examined, or projected effectively in space and over time without resorting to myth.[10] So it is urgent to intensify sociological research on this subject and to examine it much more closely.

In this spirit, this volume outlines a process of analysis that focuses mainly on the social aspects of myth: the actors who promote it, the functions it fulfils in the culture and the society, the relationships and the power strategies that influence its emergence and govern its reproduction, the meanings it takes on for individuals and groups, and the transformations it brings about or undergoes.[11] This presents a very ambitious challenge. The project on which I am embarking is intended to shed light on the social and symbolic dynamics that bring about the emergence of myths and ensure both their perpetuation and their replacement. Concentrating on the social dimension of myth, I will therefore deal only incidentally with the crucial psychoanalytic foundations in which it is rooted and from which it is sustained.

Finally, in more theoretical terms, all of these questions converge towards the general issue of the relationships (a) between the two major dimensions or spheres of culture – on one side, the structural forms, the constants, and on the other, everything derived from them: cultural codes, customs, traditions, and so on; (b) between values and behaviours; and (c) between symbolism and the social.

In short, the relevance of this volume will be shown in reference to the extremely powerful symbolic mechanisms at work here. One could argue that the rationality of the actors provides a sufficient basis to clarify all these phenomena. I postulate instead that it is above all emotion – the symbols it feeds and the motivations it drives – that, when all is said and done, orients the game.

B. The Collective Imaginaries

As indicated above, I approach the world of culture through the concept of the collective imaginary. I arrived at this choice after years of investigation in social and cultural history.

A Scientific Choice

First I did research in comparative history on a region located in northeastern Quebec (the Saguenay). The study was aimed at describing the features of French Canadian society as it was reproduced in these far-off spaces, which had been opened to settlement just before the middle of the nineteenth century. Because of the distance and isolation that usually characterized those new communities, there was even reason to believe that these features would be accentuated.

The results of my work (G. Bouchard, 1996, 1997) were received with some surprise. On many points, in fact, the empirical data flatly contradicted the image of French Canadians that had been conveyed for so long by ideologies, in novels, and in present-day representations – namely, that they were sedentary peasants, chained to rigid traditions, resistant to the market and progress, confined by a communitarian culture, and so on. More remarkable still, comparison with English Canadian provinces and regions of the United States revealed surprising similarities demographically, economically, socially, and even culturally, where marked differences would have been expected.

These conclusions drew attention primarily to the modes of production and dissemination of collective representations, especially representations of identity. They also suggested that the study of Quebec society should not be confined to the overly narrow and somewhat distorted perspective of a cultural minority of French heritage; rather, it should be opened up to the broad horizons of the continent, as a collectivity of the New World.

In a second phase, I resolved to greatly expand the scope of comparison by studying this time the formation of national identities and cultures in the collectivities of the New World – namely, the two Americas, Australia, and New Zealand. Once again, the survey revealed many similarities but also unexpected differences (G. Bouchard, 2000). One lesson I learned from all of this research was how many distortions, falsehoods, and contradictions can be introduced into the representations a society maintains and projects of itself. This in turn drew my attention to (a) the formation, structure, and reproduction of collective imaginaries, (b) the myths that sustain them, and (c) the social actors that construct them and transform them according to their world view and their interests.

Collective Imaginaries: A Definition

Very generally, and too vaguely, the concept of the collective imaginary often refers to all of the symbols that a society produces and through which its members give meaning to their lives. Defined this way, it can hardly be distinguished from the concept of culture. More specifically, the collective imaginary includes that which, in the mental universe, belongs more to the psyche than to reason per se. And more precisely still, the collective imaginary is characterized by the link it establishes between familiar realities such as norms, traditions, narratives, and identities on the one hand, and, on the other hand, the deepest symbolic structures. Collective imaginaries conceived in this way are composed of representations that draw their authority from an empirical foundation, significant experiences of a community, and non-rational roots.

The above statement is in line with the writings of Gilbert Durand, who wanted to overcome what he called "the artificial empire of reason."[12] All of his works amount to attempts to restore the entirety of the mental universe by including in it the aspect of "dreams and lies." However, I would consider it ill-advised to restrict the imaginary to the non-rational; in the construction of ideologies, the genesis of national myths, and the formation of discursive strategies, the non-rational operates but reason nevertheless plays an essential role. Durand himself recognized this in many of his writings, and we find the same idea in L. Boia (1998, pp. 60–61) and others.

My concept of collective imaginaries borrows extensively from the abundant European literature. It is also marked by a few authors (including Durand and J.-J. Wunenburger) with whom I feel a particular theoretical affinity, although I never embrace all of their arguments. What follows is therefore a personal vision fuelled by freely interpreted or reorganized references.

I believe, first of all, that we can distinguish among imaginaries the four following levels or dimensions:

1. A first dimension is that of **the unconscious**, of the psyche strictly speaking – namely, the primary forces (or the profound vital

tendencies) that govern individual and collective consciousness and that are the concern of psychoanalysis. This is the domain of impulses and impetus, instincts, deep emotions – of what H. Corbin (1958) calls the "imaginal," namely, fears, anxieties, sexual desires, appetites for domination, feelings of fault, a taste for the marvellous, the pleasure principle, the need for the sacred or transcendence (religious or not), and life and death instincts.[13]

2. At a second level, we find **the cognitive substrates** that are the deep mental structures, the great cross-cultural matrices, often ahistorical, pre-existing any context, many of which can be compared to the archetypes of Carl Gustav Jung.[14] This concept has had many definitions; I like the one proposed by C.-G. Dubois (2009): "The archetype is the unconscious foundation of a symbol, giving rise to strong affective reactions" (p. 217). Durand thus called for an analysis of the "transcendental fantastic."[15]

More concretely, archetypes are stable forms, observable in most cultures at various periods – for example, initial chaos, the search for origins, creation and the end of the world, the appeal and fear of the supernatural, the insoluble bonds of blood, the eternal return, the new-born saviour, metamorphosis, renewal or rebirth, return to the place of origin,[16] original sin, the Apocalypse (and its many secular variants such as climate or nuclear catastrophes), treason, revenge, martyrdom or sacrifice of the expiatory victim, exodus, and so on.

The cognitive substrates also include opposing pairs such as similar and different, pure and impure, diurnal and nocturnal, masculine and feminine, sin and punishment, good and evil, life and death, body and soul, and so on and so forth.[17] All of these images can be seen as being founding to the extent that (a) they give rise to other images and (b) they precede and feed the work of reason.

3. A third dimension, close to the last one, includes very common **analytical categories** that support thought, such as change–stability, break–continuity, identity–otherness, sacred–secular, centre–periphery, inclusion–exclusion polarities, and also perceptions of space, concepts of time seen as linear or cyclical, constellations of events, and so on.

4. Finally, a fourth component covers **the cultural patterns**, which are socially produced collective representations and therefore more linked to the contexts. I am thinking of visions of the self and others, of

the past and the future, as well as ideals and norms that set collective goals and guide behaviours. I am thinking too, more particularly, of discursive patterns, namely recurring configurations taking the form of repertoires (not to be confused with the cognitive substrates, which are primary images of universal scope).[18] The millenarian cycle is an example of this, with its three periods: the golden age, the decline, the reconquest (the return of the golden age). Another is the cycle of sin, atonement, and forgiveness.

Cultural patterns also include ideological constructs conceived to overcome the contradictions that every society faces at various moments in its history. Observe, however, that the solutions to these aporias are limited in number and that it is possible to list them, which, via another route, takes us back to the concept of repertoire. Finally, it is also in this fourth component that reside social myths as a particular form of cultural patterns.

These are especially influential when they are rooted in cognitive substrates and archetypes. Here are a few examples. The theme of new beginnings and renewal permeates most if not all revolutionary ideologies.[19] But this messianic theme is usually exploited in a way that evokes a road map to thrilling horizons rather than a leap into the void that would give rise to anxiety and curb zeal. In addition, the perspective of a radical change is usually eased by references to the past and elements of continuity discreetly integrated into the discourse of change. The same is true for the concept of rebirth, subject to various modulations.[20]

The image of the rupture proves effective by holding out the prospect of a better time as well as the end of a corrupt social order or a despised political regime. It also ensures a reconciliation with a painful past to the extent that it is banished by the act of rupture. But it remains deceptive because it hides an aspect of strategy: decreeing a state of rupture may favour mobilization and lead to changes favourable to those who are dominant or those who aspire to power. However, total rupture in the course of a history is impossible; an aspect of continuity is always contained therein. Even the rupture associated with the Flood, that "second birth of humanity," included an element of illusion (T. Hentsch, 2002, pp. 114–115). One can also maintain the opposite, since any tradition accommodates a succession of more or less deeply concealed ruptures.

Sometimes the image of metamorphosis, which can work backward or forward, fills an analogous function. Rather in the same vein, many societies going through difficult times have found inspiration and comfort in the biblical imagery of the Exodus (the American *Mayflower*, the migration of the Voortrekkers in South Africa, the exile of Jews from Israel and their return, etc.). The Christian millenarian tradition reproduces the images of the golden age, the return to chaos (or the descent into hell), a period of hardship and suffering, then of resurrection, and the return to the golden age. Moral reforms (associated with fascism, for example) exploit the primary figures of regeneration and purification. Dictatorial regimes promote the greatness and necessity of the virtuous hero, often sacrificed, and so on and so forth.

In short, we could say that one part of the collective imaginary is structural (the roots of meanings, symbols and primary images, structural categories), while another refers to processes (the discursive constructs, the production and promotion of meanings, images, and symbols by often competing social actors; see below).[21] From another perspective, it appears that the first part belongs mostly to the psyche (in particular, the emotions) while the second places great importance on reason (in particular, political and instrumental reason), although reason's operation is always influenced by the psyche and emotion. In this regard, the concept of the imaginary is distinguished from the Durkheimian concept of collective consciousness, which refers to a set of representations associated mainly with cultural patterns rather than archetypal forms.

Clearly, one merit of the concept of the collective imaginary is its capacity to straddle many dimensions of the cultural universe, from the psyche to cultural patterns (including norms and traditions) and social dynamics per se. It therefore includes essential elements of the theory of fields of P. Bourdieu (1986) and of the theory of social action proposed by A. Touraine (1965). This broad horizon forms the basis for the contribution of the collective imaginary to cultural sociology.

A System of Relationships and Representations

It can be said that in any society, the collective imaginary, thus construed, establishes and perpetuates eight types of representations that together form the basis for the constitutive relationships of a culture.

The reader will notice that some of these representations, though, are stronger and more stable than others:

1 **Representations of space**, by virtue of which a given geographic unit is humanized and transformed in a surveyed territory (a native land, a household, a homeland, historic sites, familiar landscapes). Such a space is inhabited and travelled, dreamed and told, and from it emerge a toponymy, legends, paintings, and so on.[22] We can recognize here the process of the symbolic appropriation of a place.
2 **Representations of time**, which is divided into days, weeks, months, and seasons, with each unit wrapped in an imagery that is a source of various emotions (we know the moment of truth, the dark hours of the homeland, holidays, the month of the dead, the season of love or vacations, the golden age, etc.).
3 **Representations of the social** by virtue of which an individual is assigned a rank or status in terms of prestige, authority, assets, and power. These representations also include the perceptions individuals have of their peers, the social structure, institutions, and authorities.
4 **Representations of the self and others**, which form the basis for an identity dynamic of inclusion and exclusion, which is expressed in an Us–Them relationship, based on various symbolic markers.
5 **Representations of the past** that feed a narrative, a collective memory, which is constructed using various materials and channels: scholarly history, novels, folk tales, museums, historical sites, heritage, documentaries, media, commemorative rituals, and so on. One fascinating aspect of this is the omnipresent need to endow oneself with a long memory even in societies emerging from relatively recent settlement, as we can see in the nations of the New World (G. Bouchard, 2000, chapter 7; 2007b). This is one way for new, fragile societies to secure for themselves a symbolic substance that allows for a sense of belonging and respect.
6 **Representations of the future** through goals or collective projects, utopias, dystopias, and the like. A sense of a mission, be it collective, providential, or other, is a common figure in these representations.
7 **Representations of the nation or society** as a whole that provide it with legitimacy and establish it as a site of allegiance that is part of a history in the making.

8 Finally, at the deepest and most general level: **representations of the universe, life and death, this world and the hereafter**, through which individuals give meaning to their existence.

Note once again that reason plays an essential role in the construction and reproduction of these representations (identities, utopias, ideologies, narratives, etc.). In this way, as mentioned earlier, products of reason – and not just the images that form their basis – also belong to the imaginary. To various degrees, however, all of these representations and relationships, rational or not, feed on myths and hence, once again, on the special attention those myths should be accorded. Because even though it is comprised of knowledge, commonsense truths, customs, codes, models of behaviour, and rules, as well as rumours, clichés, stereotypes, and other by-products of thought, the imaginary is based mainly on myths.

But before we tackle this subject, a few clarifications are required.

Diversity of Scales

First of all, an imaginary can operate at various levels, from the village to the nation, from the family to the social class. The concept also applies to the lives of organizations (businesses, sports clubs, etc.) and institutions. However, my reflections focus on the level of the society or nation.

Fiction and Reality

Unlike many authors (and most dictionaries), I maintain that collective imaginaries do not belong solely to fiction. They always have a connection with reality – a very flexible connection, obviously, and different from the one that sustains scientific knowledge.[23] I will thus avoid drawing a sharp contrast between imaginary and reality. An apparently quixotic utopia can eventually be transformed into ideologies and action programs that mobilize the masses. We can perceive social inequalities as a profound injustice and draw from them the motivation for a revolutionary project activated by myths. A painting contributes to structuring the vision of a place and making it a source of emotions. The strictly physical reality of death exists only for the scientist or the professional; for all others, it evokes a battery of images that extend beyond the materiality of death while being attached to it. A walk in the streets of Vienna can be transformed into a pilgrimage in memory of Stefan Zweig and lead to philosophical reflection or daydreaming.

In all these cases, are perception and imagination really cut off from reality? By the same token, and without falling into paradox, must not scientific knowledge of reality rely on procedures, approximations, intuitions, and images that relativize what is considered the prerogative of "real" knowledge? I therefore contend that the imaginary shapes a particular appropriation of reality that combines emotion and reason.

The Question of Coherence

Imaginaries are not necessarily coherent; in fact, they rarely are. What are most often seen in a given society are complex configurations dominated by a few powerful representations, marked by contradictions that are unevenly overcome and hidden. On the fringes of these predominant configurations, we usually find competing configurations that are likely to eventually replace the previous one or that are doomed to remain in the margins. It follows that competition, clashes, interrelationships, and change are familiar phenomena in these configurations. This means that, while imaginaries are stable in their psychological entrenchments, cognitive substrates, and analytical categories, they are in constant movement as cultural patterns.

Collective imaginaries are only partly structured. Broad segments elude the control of reason, being part of the unpredictable movement of praxis[24] and discursive strategies. As for the rational part of the imaginary, nothing justifies granting it a kind of lasting hegemony.

This being said, the fact remains that at any given moment in its history, a society (or an entire continent) is characterized by a few prominent features of civilization that form areas of coherence. I have already mentioned the "semantic basins" of Gilbert Durand, those huge symbolic configurations that irrigate constellations of cultures and prevail (while being transformed) in the very long term.[25] Similarly, islands of coherence can also be present at the microsocial level.

Agent or Product?

The definitions of the collective imaginary proposed in the literature are often ambiguous. In fact, the imaginary is presented sometimes as an active entity, a mental organization endowed with powers, the operations of which generate representations, and other times as the products of those operations.[26] Strictly speaking, the first aspect would seem to belong rather to the imagination (understood in the very broad sense), whereas its products belong to what could be called established culture.

In the following pages, I adopt this conception, with one important caveat: In its archetypical, unconscious roots, the imaginary is driven by a force it would be difficult to consider external since it operates at the level of primary images. Therefore the same ambiguity remains. So we must admit that the imaginary has two overlapping dimensions – it is both producer and product. My analysis, however, will deal mostly with the latter by emphasizing the role of social processes and discursive procedures.

The Sources of the Imaginary

The cultural patterns that comprise the collective imaginary draw from a multitude of sources. They are either discursive constructs derived from high culture or ritualized products of mass culture, among which I include the traditions and beliefs associated with what was previously called popular culture. The religious in turn overlaps these two sources, thus constituting another highly significant reservoir of symbols, in premodern as well as in contemporary societies.

Structure and Change

The concept of the imaginary is controversial in another respect. Some authors view it as a structure (e.g., as "crystallized"), while others instead pay attention to historicity and change. The definition I propose avoids this debate by stating that the imaginary is (a) structural and structuring in some of its dimensions, and (b) immersed in the social and change in other dimensions.[27]

The Individual and the Collective

It is possible to doubt the existence of the imaginary as collective reality. After all, the symbols that comprise it are all located in individual minds. Obviously, it is only metaphorically or by inference that we can speak of a collective consciousness. This being said, we cannot deny the power of the representations, norms, traditions, beliefs, and models that societies have developed in the course of their history and that they disseminate among their members.

With respect to cultural patterns, we can consider the case closed since the demonstrations of Durkheim – in particular, in his book on suicide (1951). In that work, he showed that suicide – obviously among the most individual of all acts – manifests surprising regularities, thereby following a model that attests to the hold of the collective. The social nature of cultural patterns is also confirmed by power relations and the social actors that promote them strategically as well as by collective bodies (such as institutions) that ensure their transmission.

As for archetypes, cognitive substrates, and analytical categories, their universal (or near universal) nature within each society and from one society to another proves their collective dimension and forms the basis for a sociological or anthropological approach.

But I reject the idea that the social (or the collective) is the site of a specific, supra-individual entity, the locus of a consciousness or unconscious. This hypothesis is not required to establish the collective nature of certain representations.

The Concept of the Social Imaginary

Finally, I distance myself from the concept of the social imaginary, for various reasons. First of all, it has limited scope and can lead to confusion. In fact, it usually conveys a vision of collective facts, mechanisms, and processes that does not leave enough room for important components of imaginaries, such as the psyche or cognitive substrates. However, as I have pointed out, the study of imaginaries requires us to take into account simultaneously their structural dimension, the site of founding images, and their strictly social aspect, which is the arena of power relations and agents.

C. Castoriadis (1975) makes extensive use of the concept of the social imaginary, but in a very specific way. Responding to the materialist interpretations of Marxism, he attempted to emphasize the crucial role played by individuals in the dynamics of a society. He saw the proof of their autonomy in their ability to define creatively ("imagine") their destiny and to act accordingly by remodelling the social order. From this perspective, the imaginary takes the form of a program of social change through reforms or revolutions. This is a reductive meaning of the concept.

What is more, according to Castoriadis, only modern, democratic societies offer the conditions necessary to construct a social imaginary, with the first of these conditions being the capacity for action. But he also asserts that postmodernity had destroyed those conditions. So defined, the concept of the imaginary is subject to a double restriction. It refers to a program of change in a society, and consequently to ideological choices and sociopolitical orientations; it is also limited to certain social and cultural contexts broadly associated with modernity.

For other researchers, the concept of the social imaginary does not necessarily extend to an entire society or culture, and this imposes another restriction. For example, for B. Baczko (1984), the concept refers mainly to the representations developed by totalitarian powers to establish their legitimacy as well as their domination over groups or classes. In a way perhaps even more restricted, for C. Taylor (2002, pp. 91–92, 105–107), the social imaginary excludes ideas, theories, doctrines, and visions of the world derived from high culture, unless these are disseminated to the entire population, thereby permeating mass culture. The minds of intellectuals are said to be sustained by sophisticated, articulated ideas, whereas mass mentality is said to be imbued with legends, "myths," and so on. This concept thus establishes a hierarchy within collective representations on the basis of their social referents, in such a way that certain representations are assumed to be just "imagined," while others are not.

From a methodological *and* theoretical point of view, and with respect to the imaginary as I have defined it, this kind of privilege granted to high culture is difficult to justify. Creations formalized by intellectuals are certainly very different from the content of popular or mass cultures; but the former are still based on discursive strategies that promote values, beliefs, ideals – and myths (see chapter 2). They are simply structured in a more rigorous and more refined way thanks to the demonstrating and critical work of reason.

Chapter Two

What Is a Social Myth?

In order to define social myth, it is important first of all to correct the common perception that reduces myth to fable, legend, harmless fiction, a utopian vision (the end of divisions and inequalities, a taxless society, universal peace, etc.), or to a malicious, harmful manipulation that deceives and alienates and that can lead to the most profound abuses, of which there are many examples in ancient and recent history. These are impoverished conceptions of myth that reduce it to certain of its manifestations.

Basically, a sociological perspective suggests that we consider myth as a type of collective representation (sometimes beneficial, sometimes harmful[1]), as a vehicle of what I would call a message – that is, of values, beliefs, aspirations, goals, ideals, predispositions, or attitudes. One can refer here to the myth of racial superiority or to the myth of the superior nation, chosen by God and vested with a universal mission. Other examples are the myths that support fundamentalist ideologies (religious or not) and that can lead to violence. But one can also think of the major founding myths of humanism and modernity: equality, liberty, tolerance, human dignity, democracy, and progress. So it is important not to confuse myth as a sociological mechanism with the symbolic content (or message) it can convey. Recall here also that I am referring to beliefs and values without attributing to these concepts a (positive or negative) normative weight. Once again, myth can tilt either to the side of evil or to the side of virtue.

As noted earlier, this essay is intended to provide a better understanding of this powerful mechanism, which has the capacity to send an entire society in the most diverse directions, from the purest altruism to the most destructive fanaticism.

A. Myth as Collective Representation

Six features together form the basis for the distinctive nature of myth as collective representation and as a particular way to create meanings:

An archetypal foundation. One way or another, myths are always linked to archetypes. They are rooted in them and ultimately feed off them.[2] It does not follow from this that archetypes determine social thought or action. Rather, acting as matrices, they delimit the area of invention, as we can see with national myths, which have a limited repertoire (G. Bouchard, 2013b). In other words, archetypes constitute a kind of keyboard on which representations are constructed.

By broadening the perspective, we can deduce that in any society, the imaginary designates a symbolic field within which what is not thought is in a way unthinkable. In the case of nineteenth-century Quebec, for example, how can we explain why scientific positivism, Marxism, and the major social utopias that swept across the Western world barely reached that society? We could ask the same question with regard to the model of the frontier that has permeated thinking in most new communities, or the major writings of Tocqueville on democracy. Neither of these left strong traces on the tradition of Quebec thought.

Hybridity. A myth is always an unevenly calibrated and shifting blend of reality and fiction, reason and emotion, consciousness and unconsciousness, truth and falsehood. Analysis, however, suggests that we should go beyond these dichotomies to work, so to speak, in the in-between, where the true nature of myth lies. Here I immediately point out a corollary: from a sociological perspective, a myth above all must be evaluated on the basis not of its "truth," but of its effectiveness (as we will see in chapters 3 and 4).

Many authors have adopted the former perspective, examining primarily the truth or falseness of the myth (e.g., J. Campbell, 1988; C. G. Flood, 2001; B. Lincoln, 1992; K. Schilbrack, 2002). From a strictly scientific perspective, this is a secondary dimension and perhaps a red herring – except, of course, when it comes to religious myths considered from the perspective of the believer; see, for example, R. Pettazzoni (1984). The sociologist's objective is simply to understand the functioning of that mechanism. But from the point of view of the citizen or ethics, it is, of course, very different.

Since it is the vehicle of a belief, a value, or an ideal, a mythical representation is first of all a gamble on reality or the future (world peace, freedom, democracy, equality, etc.). We can see that in its main function, the myth promotes and promises more than it reflects reality, with which it is always in tension.

Emotivity. As noted earlier, rationality intervenes in various ways in the construction of a myth and in other aspects of the imaginary. However, a well-established myth is characterized (and conditioned) by being primarily emotion-driven, which helps us understand the liberties it can take with reality and the resilience it can show when it faces contradictions.

Sacredness. A full-fledged myth draws its authority mainly from the fact that it participates in a form of sacredness and thus exists beyond the realm of rationality. This characteristic, which largely exempts it from being called into question and from being "attacked" by reality, accounts for its predominance, resilience, and longevity. The fact that a message has become unassailable can even be seen as confirmation that it has taken on the form of a myth.[3] Recall here that among the Greeks, myth (*muthos*) was speech that was beyond criticism (P. Trousson, 1995, p. 35 ff.).

Instrumentality. Originally, most social myths were constructed by competing collective bodies in situations of power relations.[4] This dimension brings out the central role of discursive strategies as procedures of communication, acculturation, and persuasion. As we will see, the instrumentality of myth does not prevent it from being internalized and experienced as authentic by the target public, which ensures its effectiveness (once again, I leave aside the question of its veracity).

Narrativity. Social myths are usually based on references to the past – namely, episodes or experiences viewed as especially significant and recorded through various procedures and channels. But it would be a mistake to reduce myth to a narrative, even though it is a significant component of narrative.

In light of these statements, the beginnings of a definition emerge: rooted in the psyche, strategically produced and used, social myth is a collective representation that is hybrid, beneficial, or harmful, imbued with the sacred, governed by emotion more than by reason, and a vehicle of meanings, values, and ideals shaped in a given social and historical environment. Among these attributes, sacredness is the most decisive, and not narrativity, contrary to what is often stated. It is sacredness that mainly distinguishes myth from all other collective representations.

As such, social myth should be considered an attribute of any society, a universal sociological mechanism. So there is no point in trying to eradicate it. We can also expect, since it affects consciousness, that myth will influence individual and collective behaviours.

This is the visible face of myth. But as mentioned above, there is also a darker, murkier aspect. Even while promoting noble ideals and expressing profound truths about a society, myth can conceal and disguise other, less honourable truths that people refuse to admit to themselves and to others. Here we are in the domain of denial, misrepresentation, and taboo, in the realm of the blind spots of thought and culture, through which a society seeks to mask its abdications, faults, denials, and failures, often by placing the blame on others – as happens with the mechanisms of victimization and scapegoating.

For example, consider the fate for a long time reserved for Native people and blacks by the United States: they were deprived of the rights that the Constitution had solemnly recognized for all citizens. However, official political discourse ignored that astonishing contradiction for generations. In the Quebec context, we could mention the constant vigilance this society exercises to protect its language. This subject has deep, strongly emotional resonances regarding identity,[5] with significant political, economic, and social ramifications. Yet people are often resistant to any debate calling into question the quality of that language, which nonetheless also touches on concrete issues.[6] Another example is anglophone Canada, which, quite rightly, makes respect for diversity and a tradition of compromise a national credo. However, the different reality of Quebec creates a kind of roadblock to this, and the francophone province is usually only referred to peripherally, for instance, in Canadian literature textbooks.[7]

As mentioned above, the approach I am proposing only indirectly touches on the psychoanalytic sphere – namely, all things that, in collective imaginaries, are located beyond rationality, the social, and everyday representations. The universe of instincts, impulses, archetypes, and mechanisms of the unconscious will therefore not be analysed as such, although it will always be present. Likewise, I leave aside the cognitive substrates that deeply structure collective representations even though, once again, they inevitably intersect with my approach in various ways. My priorities lie mainly with representations, cultural patterns, behaviours, and the social (power relations, actors and their strategies). These are the most visible face of myth, construed as social fact.

This definition of myth, combined with reference to collective imaginaries, owes much to the sociology of Émile Durkheim in that it emphasizes the importance of the symbolic foundations of a society and situates myth as part of the entire social dynamic.[8] As we will see, what this definition adds to the Durkheimian view is (a) particular attention to the conflictual, political, and strategic dimensions of the mythical construct, (b) recognition of the key roles played by emotion and archetypal structures, (c) a focus on the selective use of the past to strengthen the mobilizing symbols of a society, (d) an analytical model intended to take into account the emergence, the reproduction, and the decline of myths, and (e) the idea of a pyramidal architecture of myths within a collective imaginary (see chapters 3 and 5 on the mythification process and on master and secondary myths). Finally, my approach recognizes a key role for social actors as constructors of myths, as opposed to Durkheim, who posits that collective representations are produced globally by the society as a transcendent entity or force.

B. Specificity of Social Myths

What makes social myths specific among all the myths that make up collective imaginaries? In a Durkheimian sense, and from a very general perspective, we can state that all myths and symbols are social in that their emergence is always a product of collective life. For Durkheim, for example, the religious was a transposition or a hypostatized vision of the social, like any representation that is part of the collective consciousness. According to him, individuals internalize these representations under the effect of constraints imposed by the society. This being said, to avoid any confusion, it would be better to qualify as societal that site of collective life that, according to Durkheim, is the seat of what he calls obligatory beliefs and ritual practices – everything that is mandatory, he writes, is socially determined.[9]

But we can talk about a social myth in the strict sense of the term, emphasizing not the overall societal dynamic but, more specifically, the role of the actors, their motivations, the power relations in which they are involved, their strategic operations, and the concrete, immediate issues associated with them. To better highlight these particular features of the social myth, it can be useful to situate it in relation to other types of myth. In formal terms (but only formal), it is possible in effect to recognize, as some authors have, a typology within all myths on the basis of certain ways in which they are constructed. This effort, as we will see, encounters significant problems. So it is with reservations that I present the following classification, which, again, is based not on the specificity of the symbolic content (there is substantial osmosis from one type to another) or on the uses to which myths are put (each type can be used for very diverse purposes), but on different modes of construction.

In this regard, beyond social myths per se, four other types of myth can be identified, keeping in mind that they are not entirely cut off from the social.

Religious Myths

These myths essentially belong to the supernatural and are therefore based principally on faith – namely, on the acceptance of principles considered to be profound truths related to the most basic dimensions of life and the cosmos. I am thinking here of the divine origin of life and the universe, sin and forgiveness, the Chosen People, eternal life (the Promised Land), the Hindu *ahimsa*, and so on. These myths primarily express the foundations of religious life, manifestations of the gods in daily life, and relationships of humans with mysterious powers that are beyond them. Thus they draw their authority from the sanction of a god or a supernatural force. They have been analysed in classic studies by famous authors such as Joseph Campbell, Otto Rank, and Mircea Eliade.[10]

Philosophical Myths

These myths refer to the ontological sphere, and, without any a priori reference to the supernatural, they provide rational explanations related to the human condition, death, the purpose of the universe, the problem of good and evil, the conditions of knowledge, and so on and so forth. Pythagoras's prime numbers, Plato's metaphor of the cave, Hobbes's Leviathan, Rousseau's noble savage, Kant's moral law, Hegel's Spirit, and Nietzsche's Superman all come to mind here.

Allegorical Myths

These are myths from stories and legends, the arts, and literature.[11] Belonging to the world of fiction, they present images and fantasies sustained by mystery, by the marvellous, by ugliness and the macabre, by hopes and fears, by the tragic and the comic, by the epic and the romantic. In the literary tradition, they have provided legendary characters such as Faust, Don Juan, Don Quixote and, more contemporarily,

Dracula (and his famous castle, which continues to attract hordes of tourists). I am also thinking of the tales of chivalry – including Tristan and Isolde – and the portrait gallery of the Arthurian cycle. The major figures who populate the Greek imaginary (Aphrodite, Athena, Ulysses, Prometheus, the Minotaur, etc.) also belong to allegorical myths, as do the sports heroes celebrated today. Recall as well the big Hollywood productions that adapt to today's tastes very old themes associated with familiar archetypes.

Allegorical myths can also be embodied in fantastic images as varied as apocalyptic visions of the end of the world, the far side of the moon (before the era of space exploration), the quest for the Holy Grail, and stories of chivalry or courtly love. The statues on Easter Island, the pre-historic monuments of Stonehenge, the pyramids of Egypt, lands flowing with milk and honey, Eldorado, and the Bermuda Triangle are also among the allegorical myths, given the intense curiosity they arouse. Among more contemporary figures, one could mention the wreck of the Titanic, outer space (extra-terrestrials, UFOs), Mount Everest (unfortunately losing its appeal), Alcatraz prison, and many others.

Scientific Myths

It is tempting to extend this typology to what could be called, at least by analogy, scientific myths, namely the paradigms that form the basis for theories. These are the myths most strictly subjected to tests of reality and consistency, whether in the natural sciences (the principle of accuracy) or mathematics (the principle of logic). These myths are nevertheless based on primary propositions that are considered a priori to be true but that are rarely proven. Even so, researchers feel they have to subscribe to them to avoid being censured professionally (criticism, marginalization, denial of grants, publication, promotion, etc.). They constitute the foundation for all scientific discourse.[12]

Like social myths, scientific myths survive above all thanks to their effectiveness, which here means their capacity to produce knowledge and solve new (or very old) problems. The postulate that formed the basis of Euclidian geometry is a perfect example. This postulate, as we know, holds that through a point outside a straight line, you can draw one and only one parallel line to infinity. Indeed, it took more than two millennia for other postulates that contradicted it to appear. There was first of all the geometry of Nikolai Lobachevsky (1792–1856), according to which you can, through a point not on a straight line, draw more than one parallel line. A little later, Bernhard Riemann (1826–1866) introduced another non-Euclidean geometry according to which, through a point outside a straight line, you can draw no parallel lines. What is remarkable is that these two theories, apparently illogical, have gained acceptance; indeed, they have found many scientific and technical applications – Einstein himself founded part of his physics on Riemann's geometry.[13] Since then, many non-Euclidean geometries have appeared (one of the more recent being fractal geometry). This has become almost commonplace, and we tend to forget the huge challenges that the theories of Lobachevsky and Riemann faced to become established.

This example, like many others, shows clearly that the imaginary is never really disconnected from reality.[14] But it also highlights the fact that paradigms, as sets of shared beliefs (T. Kuhn, 1962), operate like myths. Their fate is determined not by their veracity but by their effectiveness, and their veracity is rarely proven. Beyond geometry, the same is true with the old idea of race in traditional anthropology, the idea of natural law in science (which affirms the symmetry of the universe, a reflection of divine perfection or an intrinsic order), the human as a free agent in the social sciences (or society as a living organism), the concept of the unconscious in psychoanalysis, and so on. And we could also mention the rational individual dear to many economic and sociological theories, the famous *Homo economicus* and the self-regulating market of the liberal economy (Adam Smith's famous "invisible hand"), or the supposed law of natural selection, which cannot be proven experimentally except through observation carried out over an almost limitless period of time.[15]

Paradigms, just like social myths, are founding statements that participate both in fiction and in reality, in imagination and in reason, and they eventually acquire a great autonomy thanks to a form of sacredness that grants them an immunity. They develop through their links to a praxis, and they decline when people start to see them not as false but rather as ineffective. They are then replaced by others. But the authority they enjoy and their social roots permit them to sometimes resist contradictory data for a long time.[16] The role of institutional and power strategies is also decisive.[17] Proposals for new paradigms are even accredited according to procedures similar to those that govern mythification (see the next chapter).[18]

All of this is based on the fact that the representation conveyed by the paradigm (or, should we say, the para-dogma?) is prior to the work of scientific reason per se – that it has the function of preparing, sustaining, and supporting. Remember here how Einstein's religious convictions ("God does not play dice with the universe") had an impact on his scientific thought, compromising even its fulfilment at a time when the uncertainties of the infinitely small were establishing the era of randomness and probabilities. In the same vein, P. Bourdieu (1991, pp. 331–342) brought to the fore the myth (the "fantasy," the "social unconscious") that supported Montesquieu's climate theory. It is also known that the Greek philosophers favoured balance and stability over movement and that among the latter, the circular was considered the least imperfect because it went back to the starting point.

In the same spirit, B. Lincoln (2000) made this bold statement: "If mythology is ideology in narrative form, then scholarship is myth with footnotes" (p. 209). We can also refer to J.-M. Berthelot (1988), who reminded us that the non-rational is the "bedrock" of images, ideas, or patterns of intelligibility on the basis of which knowledge establishes its bases and develops.[19]

The typology outlined above is useful in that it highlights the diverse ways in which myths are constructed as well as the distinctive nature of what I call social myths (as opposed to other myths). This being said, one should also be wary of this classification, for the following three reasons. First, as mentioned above, with reference to the symbolic content of myths, we observe many forms of interference and osmosis from one type to another. For example, religious myths borrow greatly from literary works.[20] Similarly, social myths borrow from archetypes and other images conveyed by allegorical, religious, and philosophical myths – from literature (the epic and heroic aspects), religion (divine origins, the concept of Chosen People invested with a divine mission), or philosophy (visions of the world, teleology). More generally, we can say that all social myths draw from the four dimensions of the imaginary mentioned earlier: drives and instincts, archetypes, analytical categories, and cultural patterns.

Second, no type of myth pursues goals or fulfils functions that are really exclusive to it. Religious myths make room for many other components, allegorical myths are not meant simply to distract, scientific myths are not determined solely by the pursuit of knowledge, and so on.

Third, all types of myths have some social component. In different ways and to various degrees, all maintain a relationship with divisions, conflicts, and power relations. With respect to functions, this is the case with religions, which Marx considered the "opium of the people," but which other theorists – Durkheim, for example – considered the foundation of the social. This is also the case with literature, which has always championed nations and all kinds of political regimes. The same is true with science, whose support is indispensable for major collective, civil, or military projects. More deeply, this can also be verified in the very process of constructing all of these discourses, which are never completely free of the social, as sociocritical analyses have shown, even with the most ethereal literary works.[21]

Similarly, research in sociocultural history and epistemology has clearly established that allegorical, religious, philosophical, and scientific myths always reflect in some way the social environment (hierarchies, tensions, conflicts, ideologies) in which they are born. Accordingly, one could expand to all myths the concept of social myths.

But for the sake of precision, it is also appropriate to distinguish between social myths in the strict sense and social myths in the broad sense. This is because certain myths, if I may put it this way, are more *social* than others since they are born and develop entirely in the immediate social arena, echoing its challenges, conflicts, and contradictions. Indeed, they maintain a very narrow, explicit, and systematic link with the social dynamic and contexts. They are the strategic products of social actors who very openly promote and use them, in a spirit of symbolic engineering. Their immediate purpose is to model behaviours and mobilize populations using various techniques of persuasion. To this end, they have a great capacity to influence minds thanks to the authority that stems from their sacredness.

Again, none of these factors by itself is really specific to social myths understood in the strict sense. It is their combination as well as the degree and the manner of their connection to the social and, more generally, to reality that distinguish them from other myths. Unless otherwise specified, it is these social myths – in the strict sense – that I will be referring to in the rest of this volume.

In short, the typology proposed remains useful for characterizing the various procedures for constructing myths, but we need to use it carefully, remaining wary of overly rigid compartmentalization and standardization.

Readers will note that this classification refers explicitly to neither national myths nor political myths. I see them as parts of social myths (in the strict sense), from which they are not fundamentally different. National myths have the characteristic of operating at the level of the global society, while social myths can operate on many levels, from the family to the continent (the European Union, for example). With political myths we find a particular emphasis on power relations mainly in government spheres, as was pointed out a long time ago by pioneering scholars such as L. C. McDonald (1969, p. 144) and H. Tudor (1972, p. 17), as well as many others since.

Analysts of political myths do not all share the same views regarding the meaning that should be assigned to the concept of myth, but the definitions they propose have much in common. The features that are most often underscored are the strategies of the actors (mainly political parties), the mobilizing power, the ideologically oriented narrative, relationships of domination, and the role of emotion. Regarding other aspects, the authors differ in their approaches, which are sometimes sociological, sometimes philosophical.[22]

Similar typologies have already been proposed by various authors. A. Von Hendy (2002), referring to the history of the concept of myth and the meanings it has successively assumed, recognizes (a) ideological myth, which he characterizes as a widely propagated lie (e.g., Marxism), (b) folk myth, which is sustained by stories and associated with traditional societies and which proposes a narrative of origins, (c) constitutive myth, which expresses the foundational beliefs of a society, and (d) romantic, ahistorical myth, which conveys transcendent, universal values. For reasons that have already been presented, and for other reasons I will be putting forward, I reject this classification, which conflates myth with ideology, reduces myth to a lie, confuses it with one of its vectors (the story), or identifies it with some of its dimensions (founding, archetypes).

Referring to the purposes of myths, J.-J. Wunenburger (2006, p. 64 ff.) distinguishes myths whose aims are (a) aesthetic/playful, (b) cognitive, and (c) establishing and practical (leading to action). I am more at ease with this typology, which, however, goes in a direction slightly different from mine. Close to this typology is that of J. Campbell (1970),[23] who also adopts as a classification criterion the purpose or function of myth, which leads to the following list of functions: (a) the mystical or metaphysical (to give meaning to life, to the human condition), (b) the cosmological (to make sense of the universe), (c) the sociological (to maintain the social order and ensure the integration of the individual), and (d) the psychological (to sustain personal life and adapt it to its social environment). We can see that, arriving from a different direction, this typology coincides in various ways with the one that I have presented, but it is also distinguished by the fact that the classification criterion is not the same.

There are other typologies based on function (e.g., G. S. Kirk, 1970) or on various themes (heroes, gods, new beginnings, time, and eternity).

Finally, religious, allegorical, and philosophical myths will not receive further attention in this volume, which is devoted to social myths and to the factors and mechanisms that determine their emergence, their functions, and their decline.

C. A Few Useful Distinctions

Myths and Ideologies

One must avoid confusing myths and ideologies. The latter are argumentative constructs intended to be rational and coherent: they focus on the defence of a political and social orientation and on the promotion of a course of action. Moreover, ideologies are based on the authority of myths or the symbols that represent them and through which they operate. As emotionally rooted and broadly shared visions (liberty, equality, justice, solidarity, religious beliefs, etc.), myths are the engines of ideologies, whose capacity to mobilize populations is drawn mainly from myths.

For example, the aristocracy is empowered to govern thanks to its pure blood, which is both heritage and proof of its sacred origins. People must obey the edicts of the king because they are the expression of God's will. The domination of men in the family is legitimate because they were chosen to defend its honour. The members of a nation should be trusting and helpful to one another since they are like brothers and sisters, they belong to the same family, they are united by the sacred bonds of blood. The actions of the rich are beneficial to a society because their prosperity contributes to the common good; it also attests to their value and their personal merit. The workers are right to revolt to bring an end to oppressive, unequal regimes that violate the ideal of social justice. The cooperative concept draws its value from the ideal of solidarity. And so on.[24]

In short, while ideologies belong to the strategic programming governed by reason, myths belong to emotion and symbolism. They provide the foundation that sustains ideologies.

According to J. Breuilly, while "sentiment motivates a particular journey, ideology provides a map and suggests routes" (2009, p. 442).

Following this line of thinking (which I agree with), one can wonder: What would have been the fate of communism without its messianism (its "parousia")? Or the fate of the rationalism of the Enlightenment without the promises of progress of the mind and the grand vision of the happiness of peoples? Or that of all nationalisms without the idealization of the nation in the past and in the future? The sacralization in which they drape themselves – and, therefore the work of myth – is what gives ideologies their power of persuasion and change. How else can we explain the "dramatization" (P. Ansart, 1990, pp. 189–190) in which rational political thought wraps itself? Conversely, ideologies have proven themselves effective vehicles for the propagation and accreditation of the myths they rely on.

This view of the relationship between myth and ideology is congruent with those put forward by various authors,[25] but it also differs from many other propositions. For example, for C. G. Flood (2001, chapter 1), ideology is distinguished from myth by the fact that it is not a narrative. This position is based on a definition of myth that I reject. In my view, myth uses a narrative, but this is not its primary characteristic. Similarly, according to P. Bourdieu (1991, pp. 205, 208–209), ideology is the product of a specific dissemination activity, while myth, which has a much broader scope, is the undifferentiated product of the entire society. I believe rather that myth is most of the time the product of a social actor or a coalition of actors. It is only at the end of a long process of promotion that it can extend its influence to an entire society. Finally, according to P. L. Berger & T. Luckmann (1967, pp. 122–134), myths are more fragile than ideologies. I take exactly the opposite view.

Myth also differs from ideology in that it is presented as a site of virtue and consensus, as an ideal that rises above the fray, supposedly exempted from challenge. Ideology, on the other hand, is very often at the centre of controversy because of the program of action it is proposing in opposition to other programs and interests. Accordingly, different, even contradictory, ideologies can claim to be inspired by the same myth. For example, liberalism and socialism both promise equality. In the United States, Republican and Democratic discourses both appeal to the American Dream and American exceptionalism, and so on.

The same can be said for utopias, those great collective dreams that, by projecting well beyond reality, describe what a society could or should become ideally – which means that utopia often remains, according to Jean Bodin, a republic in idea only, without effect. With some differences, the same remark applies to philosophical, theological, novelistic, and historiographical systems or constructs. All are sustained by myth and contribute to reinforcing it by mobilizing minds according to specific processes. There is an analogous relationship between myth and identity. In this case, however, the former feeds the latter but remains distinct. In this sense, myth is not part of what we perceive – it is what we perceive *through*.[26]

All of this goes to show that it would not be possible to do a history of ideas or ideologies without taking into account the structuring action of myths that gives them impetus and great power of persuasion and mobilization. Yet this close relationship is often ignored, as if reason alone could explain the enthusiasm and often the excesses aroused by ideas. In other words, it is myths, much more than ideas or ideologies, that "rule the world." This suggests that behind every influential idea we should look for the myth that supports it. Here we could paraphrase La Rochefoucauld by declaring that, in ideology, the use of myth is the homage that reason pays to its opposite.

Myths and Stereotypes

Myth is also distinguished from stereotype. Stereotype, like myth, has a very loose relationship with reality (e.g., by generalizing from a few often isolated cases) and owes its resilience to the irrational aspect it incorporates. It can also be used by one social actor against another actor or social group, and it can be used to buttress a myth (the stereotype of the degenerate Jewish exploiter was used in Nazi and Soviet myths). But its authority is never elevated to the rank of sacredness (you do not sacrifice your life for a stereotype); at the same time, it never takes the form of a taboo. Finally, unlike myth, it is almost always pejorative.

Similarly, moral standards and broad principles have strong authority, but they should not be confused with myth. They are, however, derived from ideals, values, and beliefs that myth conveys and promotes by elevating them to sacredness. As for fables and legends, they are innocuous narratives that are infused with the marvellous or the horrible, and they make no claims to being other than diversions, which is why they are not taken seriously – except by children. For them, I use the term "legendary."

Myths and Clichés

Another confusion arises from using the concept of myth to designate what belongs simply to cliché, metaphor, caricature, ritual, or custom.

This is the case with many of the symbols studied by R. Barthes (1972) such as "steak and chips," a photograph of a soldier, a detergent, a toy, a tourist guide, and similar phenomena that are called "mythical" – which led this author to say that "everything can be a myth." Obviously, this statement can only be verified if, by virtue of a strictly semiotic process, we identify myth with the signs or symbols that are supposed to represent it.[27] On this basis, it can, in fact, be affirmed that myth is not defined by its contents or by its sacredness, and that it refers ultimately to a dominant ideology or to popular imagery. This is far from my conception.

Finally, we need to clearly differentiate myth from the vectors that disseminate it – that is, all forms of discourse (literature, arts, media, ideologies, philosophical systems, religious rhetoric, and so forth). Among all these channels, literature has been one of the most influential, as has been shown for the United States (R. Slotkin, 1973; S. Bercovitch, 1978; R. Chase, 1980), but also for France, Germany, and many other societies.[28]

The Evolutionary Vision

As clearly shown by the above, I reject definitions of myth inspired by an evolutionary vision. I challenge the notion – which is very widespread in classical and even current anthropological literature, and also among various more recent authors[29] – that myths are characteristic of premodern societies and were eclipsed in the West as the Enlightenment progressed. According to various authors (e.g., G. Balandier, 1962; F. Dumont, 1974, p. 52 ff.), ideology and rational thought have replaced myth. I suggest rather that reason and myth form a very old couple that through the ages has maintained a succession of relationships and changing balances. Myth is therefore just as active today as in the past, but mainstream thinking seems no longer aware of it and has taken the dangerous gamble of ignoring it. This statement leads to a corollary: there was reason in so-called primitive cultures as well and in their particular modes of thinking – something that C. Lévi-Strauss (1963) recognized.[30]

I could cite many authors to illustrate this evolutionary bias, which dismisses premodern societies and views Western thought as the end result of a long process of advancement, of demythification, on which its superiority is supposedly based. Among all these authors, the great philosopher Ernst Cassirer stands out as one of the most representative, especially in his posthumous book *The Myth of the State* (1946). But there are many others, including some of the most distinguished thinkers in the West, for example, K. R. Popper (2002).

In *The Myth of the State*, Cassirer declared that myth, as fiction and/ or deception, had prevailed in the past because reason, and in particular science, was lacking. The Enlightenment and its heritage, fortunately, remedied this, hence the triumphant appearance of reason over the past two centuries. But then, after being eradicated, myth, against all expectations, reappeared in the middle of the twentieth century, in particular in the form of ultranationalism, including Nazism. Cassirer found this surprising, all the more so given that the new myths seemed to him to be the product of a deliberate construct (he could have said "rational") and therefore artificial – thus suggesting that the old myths were somehow natural. And he imputed this resurgence to three thinkers who alone, according to him, altered the course of progressive thought in the Western world: Carlyle (the myth of the hero), Gobineau (the myth of race), and Hegel (the myth of government). As if the evolution of ideas, left to its own devices, could account for very profound phenomena that disrupt symbolic, collective foundations and that activate entire societies, thus propelling them to extreme destinies. In short, Cassirer blamed failures of reason where he should have observed the ongoing actions of myth and the deep structures of the imaginary. In addition to this, he asserted that the initiatives of a few thinkers were responsible for this radical reorientation – an idea that is not very credible.

For his part, M. Eliade (1960, chapter 1) agreed that myth was present in the modern world, but he characterized it as a holdover from the primitive period. He gave as examples national flags, New Year's Eve parties, and other rituals, which he saw as debased or repressed forms of old myths. He went even further by stating that if modern representations or symbols have no precursors in ancient societies, they cannot be called myths. He could not come to terms with the idea that modern myth has an existence in and of itself.

Myths and Rituals

Finally, many authors have examined the relationships between myth and ritual. According to a tradition of research that was once highly influential (identified with the anthropological school of Cambridge, England – a school that itself was rooted in the evolutionary theories of James G. Frazer), rite in premodern societies preceded and transcended myth. This was also the opinion of Ernst Cassirer.[31] Rite could even precede the religious, in that it acquired in itself a great power simply by being repeatedly acted out. Such rituals were also considered to be stable and permanent, whereas the stories the myths attached to them varied with the storytellers and the contexts. The function of myths was to add to ritual performance an oral dimension that explained its meaning. However, rite could also disappear, with the myth enduring as a slightly impoverished vestige, a shell emptied of its original substance.[32]

I reject this representation of myth and rite that (a) gives precedence to ritual practices at the expense of the meaning of the myth, (b) asserts that myth, because of its supposed state of dependence, would not exist without the support of rite, and (c) institutes a one-to-one, organic relationship between rite and the religious. I subscribe to a more contemporary perspective that considers rite and myth as independent of each other, associated with specific functions but often interacting closely. In addition, this theoretical tradition is simplistic in that it equates myth with story and closely associates myth and ritual with the religious. I maintain instead that ritual takes its meaning from myth. In return, it helps strengthen and renew it.

D. The Definitions of Myth in the Scholarly Literature

To better highlight the definition of myth I have just presented, it is useful to provide a quick overview of the literature on this subject. During my readings in preparation for this book, I reviewed no fewer than 138 definitions of myth proposed mostly by European and North American authors, belonging to various periods. Since it is impossible to discuss them all here, I have organized them into twenty-seven categories, bringing out the spirit of each grouping. I have avoided using the typology presented above, for it would add little to what we already know. Instead I have used as classification criteria the rationales of the definitions and their theoretical roots. This exercise will also be useful to better highlight the nature and scope of the choices I have made.

The following review is based on the element given by each author as being the main trait of myth, the one on which the main emphasis was placed and that is supposed to be the basis of its distinctive character. Various authors have mentioned two, three, and sometimes four elements they consider essential, for a grand total of 201. Because of various affinities among the definitions, the classification contains inevitable overlaps. Below I briefly describe the types of definitions in order of frequency, or number of occurrences of the elements (rather than of the definitions themselves).

More Than 15 Occurrences

1 Myth is ahistorical. It reproduces major archetypes that, according to some authors, can be reduced to a single founding image. For Joseph Campbell, for example, all myths derive from a "monomyth" that recounts the fall and resurrection of the human race.
2 Myth is a lower form of knowledge (or consciousness) characteristic of primitive societies. With the progress of civilization, it was supplanted by ideology, science, and other rational discourses. We can recognize here the evolutionary, Eurocentric orientation of classical anthropology and of many contemporary authors.
3 Myth is defined essentially in reference to the religious; one way or another, it always talks about gods. Mircea Eliade is a central figure here, as are many anthropologists and philosophers.

11 to 15 Occurrences

4 Myth provides meanings, visions of the world, cosmogonies. Its main function is to dissipate anxiety when faced with the unknown, and mystery.
5 Myth is a narrative that relates remarkable events from which we can take lessons.

8 to 10 Occurrences

6 Myth explains origins, in particular those of the universe; it talks about creation, it is always foundational. This perspective is associated mainly with studies of premodern collectivities.
7 Myth is always made up of distortions and lies. It is not very credible, but it is found in all imaginaries.
8 Myth is a straightforward fiction, entertaining, taking the form of fables, stories, and legends.
9 Myth can become a malicious, dangerous discourse that inspires fundamentalist convictions and destructive behaviours. Originally,

this definition was largely associated with accounts of Nazism. It has since been extended to all forms of extremism. This is myth as a vector of alienation and as mystification.[33]

5 to 7 Occurrences

10 Myth is universal in that it occurs in all societies, primitive or modern, with primary, unchanged characteristics (the authors differ on the nature of these characteristics).
11 Myth is a vehicle for values, beliefs, and ideals that guide individuals and societies.
12 Myth is a powerful discourse that invites us first of all to question its truth or its falseness.
13 Myth is a product of unconscious impulses. This is the psychoanalytic approach, with all its variants.
14 Myth provides its meaning through the lasting relationships that structure its components. Readers will recognize here the structuralist tradition.
15 Myth is a symbolic configuration intended to resolve contradictions.
16 Myth is an overly polysemic concept. It is indefinable, confused, and perhaps unnecessary.

1 to 4 Occurrences

17 Myth is primarily social in nature. It results from processes of collective life. These definitions are above all in the Durkheim tradition.
18 Myth is born of ritual, with which it permanently maintains a close relationship.
19 Myth establishes a transcendence, a sacredness that does not necessarily belong to the religious.
20 Myth is defined by its function. Its features are deduced from the social context in which it operates and the needs it contributes to meeting. Its effect is to maintain social cohesion and balance with the natural environment.
21 Myth designates all collective representations (beliefs, world views, norms, etc.) that are deeply internalized and taken for granted.
22 Myth is a set of representations that societies develop in an attempt to overcome periods of crisis.

23 Myth features transcendent representations that arbitrate power relations and that dictate both political programs and behaviours.
24 Myth is a collective representation conveyed mainly through emotion.[34]
25 Myth acquires its distinctive nature from its capacity to mobilize populations and incite them to action.
26 Myth is a discourse that leads to alienation and thus establishes the domination of one class or one nation over another.
27 Mythical representations are the simple product of strategies of intensive communication.

Readers can see that the definitions that include the most authors or mentions (more than eleven occurrences) share a reference to "ancient" populations. Other mentions, quite numerous, have as a backdrop modern societies and come mainly from novelists, philosophers, and semioticians. Moreover, the absence of references to social actors is noticeable.

The definition I have adopted repeats in full a number of these elements (10, 11, 15, 17, 19, 21, 24, 25, and 27). It also retains certain aspects of elements 4, 5, 10, 13, 18, and 23. On the whole, it takes its specificity from their combination. Among all the authors involved, those whose approach is closest to mine are G. Sorel (1999), W. L. Bennett (1980), L. Honko (1984), R. Girardet (1986), M.-D. Perrot, G. Rist, and F. Sabelli (1992), L. Kolakowski (1989), C. Bottici (2007), and H. Fisher (2008), as well as, in particular, S.-S. Jo (2007, pp. 35–41, 163–181). I find among these authors many factors that are key to my definition. Finally, readers will forgive me for not providing a detailed discussion of all the definitions that have just been mentioned, combined with a review of the theoretical families to which they belong; I would have to devote a whole book to this, and it is not my purpose here. Besides, this kind of overview is already available in many versions.[35]

E. Myth and Reason: A Pair to Be Reconciled

The approach I am proposing is intended to rehabilitate myth as an essential component of thought. The history of the relationship between myth and reason shows that, since Antiquity, myth has taken a back seat, when it has not been quite simply rejected. But it has persisted and today demands our attention more than ever. To gain a better understanding of the following chapters, it is worth offering a brief summary of the history of this relationship.

Unsurprisingly, it all began with the Greeks. For many authors, Greek thought was structured around the opposition between *logos* (more or less the equivalent of reason) and *mythos,* which was disqualified by certain philosophers who saw it as fabrication, as a source of confusion, whereas others acknowledged its usefulness. For example, it is often remembered that Plato (like Thucydides) condemned the Homeric myths, considering them ridiculous and immoral. The Stoics, however, defended them, seeing them as useful metaphysical allegories. In contrast to this vision, which was considered too simplistic, some authors (e.g., B. Lincoln, 2000; C. Bottici, 2007, p. 21, passim) have asserted that the *logos*/*mythos* dichotomy was not so clear-cut and that Plato himself made room for myths in the structure of his thought. Writers have also pointed out that for some philosophers, rational thought was rooted in myth.

In any case, the fact remains that under the influence of thinkers such as Parmenides (father of the principle of non-contradiction), Heraclitus, Aristotle, and many others, the dissociation of reason and myth – to the detriment of the latter – is part of the heritage of Greek thought in the West. In effect, an enduring tradition has been established that condemns myth as a source of knowledge and that rejects it for propagating a false, deceptive, and degrading discourse.[36]

Later, with the growth of Catholic philosophy and science in the West (after a long detour to the Middle East), reason increased its hold on minds. The creation of universities – for example, the one in Bologna in the twelfth century – had much to do with this; so did the return to Aristotelian thought and the lasting influence of a few theologians such as Thomas Aquinas and Joachim of Flora.

This long evolution, which speeded up with the Renaissance, culminated in the Enlightenment, which, starting in the seventeenth and eighteenth centuries, established a veritable myth of reason, in the sense defined above – it was, in fact, as Chesterton said, an act of faith in the unlimited intellectual capacities of man. Reason, formerly the protector of faith, now turned against it. As for imagination, that "folle du logis" ("madwoman of the house," Malebranche), it would be subdued by critical reasoning, which was dedicated to taking control of all lower forms of consciousness – namely, everything belonging to the realm of the irrational: emotions, passions, legends, superstitions, prejudices, delusions, and, of course, myths, the supreme form of obscurantism.

Building on Descartes, Newton, Spinoza, and others, the new rules of knowledge would usher in an era of unprecedented progress. In fact, a new myth was being born, the most powerful perhaps of the modern period: all mental activities could and should abide by the standards of reason. The result of this has been extraordinary advances for Western societies. *Sketch for a Historical Picture of the Progress of the Human Mind* (1793–1794) by Nicolas de Condorcet attested to this bold program, thanks to which, it was supposed, the human race would finally leave barbarism behind.

The myth of reason survives to this day, but it has had many setbacks. Even when that myth was at its peak, reason had to deal with significant vestiges of the old regime in the form of an onerous legacy of beliefs, traditions, and "perversions" such as witchcraft, esotericism, fantasy, astrology, and alternative therapies. The old myths of Christianity still held sway, rooted in the deep culture of Western populations (the cycle of sin and forgiveness, suffering and the Second Coming, fall and redemption, death and Eden, creation and the end of the world, etc.).

At the same time, and often within or close to Christianity, major founding myths took root, such as the free, responsible individual, master of his destiny, human dignity, sovereignty of the people, the chosen people, equality, democracy, tolerance, superior races and civilizations, and great eschatological visions that promised peoples glorious, unprecedented futures.

By the late eighteenth century, the empire of reason had been shaken. Romantic currents expressed protests of affectivity (*pathos*), while classicism gave way to the Gothic, Baroque, and Rococo. Here and there, the rational was also showing its limitations. The French Revolution, which was viewed as the great political culmination of the Enlightenment, had to, under Robespierre, embrace the religion of Reason. In the social sciences, the sociologist Auguste Comte, the founder of positivism, resigned himself to extending his general theory to a "religion of humanity." Saint-Simon did likewise with what he called the "New Christianity."

Other representatives of positive science followed suit, heralding the trial of reason. Philosophers such as Giovan Battista Vico, Rousseau, Kierkegaard, and Schelling denounced the excesses of rationality.

At the same time, Freud and Nietzsche explored the abysses of the soul and Impressionism took over from Romanticism, which would soon culminate in Surrealism, which was nothing less than a desecration of natural reason and its balances. Symbolist poets such as

Rimbaud, Verlaine, and Baudelaire had already restored the domain of dream, and imagination was becoming the "queen of faculties" (Baudelaire). Moreover, the era that presented itself as the golden age of triumphant reason, it should be recalled, coexisted with the explosion of fanatical nationalisms that would wreak havoc in Europe, culminating in Nazism and the Shoah. For Stefan Zweig and many other European humanists of his generation, the two world wars represented the most bitter defeat of reason. All in all, there is nothing surprising about the rather iconoclastic argument of A. Von Hendy (2002), according to whom the time that is considered to be the era of the hegemony of reason could in fact be the era of myth.

Finally, even in pure science, the kingdom of natural law and reason had to deal with the asymmetry of the universe, which is characterized by features of relativity, relationships of uncertainty, paradoxes of causality, and other anomalies.

Another thread, that of the emergence of nations in the nineteenth century, illustrates the decline of rationalism in Europe and elsewhere. The construction of national identities – that is, the mobilization of masses around symbols of belonging, memory, and solidarity – required an appeal to emotion and myth. How could the work of reason alone operate effectively on populations with low literacy levels? And even where education was most advanced, whether to promote the nation or to raise the consciousness of the working classes, how could the masses be aroused and rallied in a lasting way, except by speaking to their hearts as much as to their minds?

The critical tradition of rationalist myth intensified during the first decades of the twentieth century (in particular, with Bergson), and especially after the Second World War. In Germany, this tradition had begun a century earlier. It reached its height with the thinkers of the Frankfurt School (Adorno, Horkheimer, Fromm, Benjamin, and others), whose consciences had been troubled by the horrors of the Shoah (O. Ombrosi, 2007). To these names, we can add those of Husserl, Cassirer, Wittgenstein, P. Ernst, Broch, Bloch, and so on. These philosophers acknowledged the indispensable role of reason but also the need to go beyond it – or beneath it.

Closer to us, in Europe and elsewhere, many voices expressed similar thoughts. I am thinking of Herbert Marcuse, the Mexican Octavio Paz, the American historian Hayden White, and even experts in business management such as J. G. March & J. P. Olsen (1975), who tried to include the irrational and contradictory dimension in their models.

It should also be recalled that for time immemorial, original minds have distanced themselves from the empire of reason. This was the case, for example, with Miguel de Cervantes, Erasmus, Rabelais, Montaigne, Giordano Bruno, Pascal, and La Bruyère (who, in his "Characters," said of reason that "only one way leads to it, but a thousand roads can lead us astray"), not to mention David Hume, who said that reason is the slave of the passions (*A Treatise of Human Nature*).

In Quebec, this critical voice has also been heard. With his plea for delinquent thought and paradoxical logics, H. Fisher (2004) is one of these critics of Western rationality. The same can be said of L.-M. Vacher (2002), P. Vadeboncoeur (2002), and, to some extent, B. Lacroix (1982, p. 113), who called for a rehabilitation of imagination.

It is clear that myth and the irrational have never lost their hold; they have simply been repressed, with the results we are all familiar with. To this day, they are manifested in religions, national identities, arts and literature, and commemoration rites, but also in their excesses and aberrations: fundamentalisms, ultranationalisms, all forms of intolerance, parallel knowledge, stereotypes, and other deviations of thought.[37]

If there is one lesson to be drawn from the foregoing, it is that it would be unrealistic to attempt to eradicate the irrational. Imagination, dream, the search for the absolute and the wonderful, beliefs and ideals, the quest for identity, sensitivity, emotions, and passions all belong to human nature and, like all human faculties, can contribute both to its abasement and to its fulfilment. The most reasonable course of action is to acknowledge and work to better understand the functioning of the human mind, which is always torn between conscious and unconscious, between reason and passion.[38]

Various avenues open up in this direction: those of psychoanalysis, psychology, and philosophy, among others. They can be found in particular in research streams on the imaginary in Europe, mainly in France. In my case, I have chosen to explore the social aspect, which belongs to sociology, and to focus my investigation on myth. However, while acknowledging the old opposition between myth and reason, I consider that myth itself, in its discursive dimension, is open to reason. Indeed, myth seeks the support of reason to ensure its advancement and reproduction (construction of ethos and narrative, accreditation, etc.; see chapter 3). This being said, the emotional component obviously remains predominant. That is why I approach myth as a sacralized composite of emotion and reason that is rooted in the psyche, imbued with transcendence, and manifested in the social.

The myth–reason pair (to return to the agreed terminology) has always existed, as pointed out by G.-G. Granger (1996, p. 31, passim), and we now know they are indissociable; indeed, that pairing is the foundation of any act of consciousness and any system of thought. All of this is an argument for a new alliance of myth and reason. This is the goal pursued by Gilbert Durand throughout his career, as well as by many other researchers.[39]

It should therefore be understood that this book is not an attack on reason, far from it. It identifies with a significant scientific current in search of a middle path, a balance that would give proper recognition to the main driving forces of the human mind and that would provide reason with the best possible working conditions, as it were.

Chapter Three

The Mythification Process

My approach focuses mainly on the social aspect of myth, that of the actors, contexts, power relations, and change, as opposed to the psychological or archetypical aspect, that of constants and universalizing forms. This raises the following question: Through what path of development and mechanisms do social myths emerge in a collectivity? Two supplementary questions concern their method of reproduction and the circumstances that bring about their decline.

According to the model I am proposing, social myths are usually the product of a mythification process – not to be confused with mystification – that involves no fewer than eight elements that contribute to shaping a powerful message.[1] What follows is a reconstitution based in part on theory and in part on empirical observation from the results of various studies, mainly in the fields of sociology, history, and communications.

A. The Construction of the Subject

Mythification presupposes first of all the construction or identification of a subject: Who are we talking about? Who is the mythical discourse intended for? This operation may seem simple, but it often runs into significant problems. In this regard, countries such as Sweden, Norway, Iceland, Portugal, Brazil, and Australia, and many others, offer an image of consistency and stability. Things are different with a few populations or communities in the New World whose geographic boundaries are uncertain and controversial. This is the case, for example, with Acadia and Puerto Rico. It is also the case with many nations in the Old World, in particular those that are engaged in or have recently been engaged in a process of territorial redefinition as a result of dismantling, merger, expansion, or conquest. I am thinking here of the two Germanies, post-Soviet Russia, Great Britain, and Israel, as well as, on another level, the European Union.

Finally, we also know of many examples of symbolic redefinition. This is the case with nations going through a process of deep identity renewal, such as Quebec and English Canada starting in the 1960s, and Poland, Great Britain, Greece, and Germany over the past two decades. These remarks also apply at the subnational level (classes, regions, parties, etc.).

B. Anchors

The second element refers to an event or to a sequence of structuring events occurring in the recent or distant past that play the role of anchors. This is the meaning that is usually given to the concept of founding myth. An anchor refers to an experience seen as decisive; very often it is a misfortune, a traumatic event (natural catastrophe, military defeat, dictatorial regime, colonial oppression, etc.). But it can also be a happier, positive experience, such as the overthrow of a despot, major humanitarian reforms, a military victory, or the founding of an empire.

However, an anchor rarely imposes itself. It usually results from a choice made by social actors among various possibilities, in the name of a group or an entire community. It is understood that in any society, the past offers many choices of anchors, many of which can remain untapped, most often because they do not match the message that social actors want to promote. In this spirit, L. P. Spillman (1997) showed the strategic nature of the episodes chosen to be commemorated in Australia and in the United States when those two nations celebrated their centenaries.

Anchors can be based on events that are both traumatic and achievements. This is the case, for example, in the United States, where the founders' experience of intolerance and rejection in Great Britain was sublimated through the episode of the *Mayflower* and the creation of a new Jerusalem. Just as, in France, the oppression associated with the Ancien Régime was erased by the revolution of 1789.[2]

With respect to traumatic events, one might be surprised that a humiliating or distressing anchor – a synonym of dispossession, and sometimes even cowardice or treason – would be chosen to feed an imaginary. In fact, this option has an advantage, since this type of reference makes it possible to initiate the millenarian myth with its triad (mentioned above) of the golden age, the fall, and the redemption. A symbolic impulse is thus created that has a mobilizing effect by providing a direction for future collective action.[3]

Moreover, according to S. J. Mock (2012a), the choice of a traumatic event as anchor corresponds to the need to clearly mark the end and even the destruction of the golden age (the first period in the millenarian cycle) so that the nation can be established. In this way, the commemoration carries out the sacrificial act that makes it possible to keep under control the violence that lies at the heart of every nation. When the ideal society of the beginning was put to death, violence was channelled towards it, which ensured the survival of the nation. This psychoanalysis-based approach is drawn from the scapegoat theory made famous by René Girard and a few others.

Dormant Anchors

We know of many cases in which it has been impossible to exploit a traumatic anchor event for memory purposes, often because of structural factors or power games. For example, the massacre of thousands of Polish officers by the Soviets in 1940 in the Katyn Forest has remained for a long time a dormant anchor (D. Bartmanski & R. Eyerman, 2011). A similar phenomenon occurred in Greece with respect to the civil war of 1946–49 (N. Demertzis, 2011). In Israel, almost two millennia went by before the Zionist movement exploited the battle of Masada in which, early in the Christian era, the Romans crushed a Jewish revolt. The strange silence in Lithuania surrounding violence against Jews during the last world war could also be considered surprising (E. Cassedy, 2012).

One could also see an anchor waiting to be "awakened" among the francophone minorities of western Canada, who have been deprived of their status as members of a founding nation with the growth of multiculturalism and the split with Quebec neonationalism since the 1960s. Another spectacular example of quasi-amnesia is the Rape of Nanking, a massacre perpetrated in China in 1938 by Japanese soldiers. It was one of the worst episodes in history of mass extermination (300,000 victims, according to various estimates), but it has scarcely entered the official Chinese imaginary until recently,[4] even though it has been dubbed the "forgotten holocaust of the Second World War" (I. Chang, 1997, pp. 5–6).[5] Being a construct, cultural trauma can thus also be a matter of choice, as N. J. Smelser (2004) has pointed out.

Closer to home, the history of the Saguenay (a region in northeastern Quebec) provides a striking example of a dormant anchor. In 1918, the Canadian army sent a detachment of several hundred heavily armed men there. Their mission was to capture young men who were fleeing conscription. For several weeks, the soldiers combed the towns and villages, bursting into houses or lumber camps in the night and terrorizing the region. Thanks to the solidarity that united all sectors of society, the population was able to organize itself to thwart the plans of the troops, and the military operation ended in failure. After the soldiers departed, the region held huge celebrations for many days. Yet this remarkable episode of regional history is today completely absent from the collective memory.[6]

Similar to what we find in genetics, there seem to be recessive anchors that can be manifested occasionally or, for various reasons, remain latent.[7]

Dormant or developing anchors can also be vehicles of positive memories. This seems to be the case currently in Quebec with the episode of the "Filles du Roy," who were sent as immigrants to New France between 1663 and 1673. The European population of the St Lawrence Valley was very much male at the time, and wives needed to be found for the young colonists. The arrival of the "Filles du Roy" was the theme of a historical reconstitution in Quebec City in August 2013, as part of the Fêtes de la Nouvelle-France (New France Festival). This remembrance received a lot of media coverage and resulted in a new narrative with feminist overtones: those young women were said to have exercised great freedom by choosing their husbands, imposing their language (French), and sowing the seeds of a form of matriarchy. Because of their contribution to the demographic growth of New France, they were also called "mothers of the nation." Some wrote that without them, New France would have died out.[8]

Finally, anchors do not necessarily belong to the past; they can also lie in the future, as anticipated utopias or dystopias. This is the case with the "eco-myth" that predicts potential catastrophes (destruction of the planet, the anger and vengeance of Mother Nature, or even divine punishment).[9] The promotion of world peace under the threat of nuclear weapons functions in the same way (consider the novel and film *The Road*). In either case, however, the discourse can also be based on effective antecedents (tsunamis, Hiroshima, Nagasaki, etc.).

Active Anchors

At the other end of the spectrum, among the anchors that have been extensively and efficiently exploited for a long time, one can mention the revolutions of 1789 in France and October 1917 in Russia, the reunification of Italy by Garibaldi, the nightmare of Soviet despotism in the countries of Eastern Europe, the landing of the *Mayflower* and the American War of Independence, the experience of slavery in many African countries, the national revolutions of the nineteenth century in many Western countries, the deportation of the Acadians in 1755, and the 1760 Conquest of Quebec by British troops (an event that has since fuelled a myth of reconquest among francophone Quebecers).

C. Imprints

Experience that is raised to the rank of anchor leaves in the collective consciousness an imprint that takes the form of a profound, lasting emotion. In the case of a negative anchor, emotion is very often fuelled by a wound and is expressed as suffering and mourning (the history of the Jews and Israel seems emblematic of this). It sometimes takes the form of a feeling of guilt that triggers a search for forgiveness, as we have seen with post-Nazi Germany. For different reasons, this is a bit similar to what is observed in South Korea, whose contemporary memory is haunted by the many defeats and humiliations that have marked the history of that country and that generate feelings of shame. This self-flagellation arises from a conviction that Koreans lacked courage and honour in the face of adversity, that they are even more to blame than their oppressors and conquerors.[10]

On the other hand, in the case of a positive experience, emotion can produce feelings of confidence, self-esteem, and power, as attested often by the example of the heirs of (even fallen) empires.[11] This being said, we also know of many cases in which attempts have been made to erase the discomfort of a negative anchor by wrapping it in a gratifying discourse.[12]

It should be understood that the feeling created by an imprint, as with all collective emotions, is largely a social construct, as demonstrated by W. M. Reddy (2001) and others. Accordingly, this feeling can be sustained and used for strategic purposes by social actors. We can refer here, among others, to R. D. Petersen (2011), who studied the Balkan wars after the breakup of Yugoslavia. There we saw ("ethnic") leaders exploit feelings of fear, anger, shame, and frustration to sway the masses, to prepare them to support or sabotage peace plans. Clearly, the relationship between anchor and imprint is flexible and cannot always be predicted.

Thus the concept of imprint opens a very wide avenue for the study of emotions as sources of motivations, collective representations, and behaviours, as called for by J. C. E. Gienow-Hecht (2010).

D. Ethos

The fourth element of the mythification process consists in the translation of the imprint into an ethos, understood as a set of aspirations, beliefs, principles, values, ideals, moral standards, visions of the world, and attitudes, or deep predispositions. For example, it is possible for a strong sense of injustice (imprint) linked to some experience of colonization or domination (anchor) to generate a quest for equality, equity, and democracy. An episode of collective humiliation is likely to generate a valorization of pride, a constant quest for respect. Similarly, we can expect the experience of slavery to foster a devotion to racial equality and human dignity. Just as a nation that was the victim of despotism will discover a strong attachment to freedom and a distrust of collective authority (or government centralization). Another nation that had been subjected to a regime of informing and spying will be very sensitive to the protection of privacy. A society that has survived civil war or a period of intense conflict will be particularly sensitive to values of unity and solidarity.[13] A small minority nation that has resisted assimilation will be naturally concerned for its survival and will want to promote values of unity, integration, loyalty, solidarity, and consensus. A nation that believes it lacked courage during an ordeal (invasion, war, natural disaster) will want to overcome its shame or its remorse with spectacular achievements, with a compensating desire for individual and collective betterment.

This being said, all of these anchors and imprints can also be fuelled by contrary predispositions, prompting resentment, hatred, desire for vengeance, and violence.

Here are a few more concrete illustrations of the anchor–imprint–ethos sequence, drawn from contemporary history:

- Gender equality is the heritage of a long history of domination and exploitation of women by men, sanctioned by the three major theist religions. Quebec, where the Catholic clergy abused its powers by treating women as inferior, is a prime example.

- The reservations (others would say the abhorrence) shown by the French republic with respect to permitting expressions of ethnocultural diversity and expressions of religion in public institutions should be understood, at least in part, in light of the great founding myths of the republic. These myths are fundamentally resistant to differences in the treatment of people; they are also deeply attached to the ideal of equality and uniformity of rights, a reflection of the hatred of the privileges and inequalities that were the impetus for the 1789 revolution. This ideal was extended to the point that rejections of inequality and of differences of rights created discomfort with ethnocultural differences. In the same way, the valorization of secularism is due in large part to a long past of intolerance and oppression associated with religion.
- The ideal of racial equality is rooted in the narratives of suffering caused by slavery and all forms of racism.
- The strong concern for national unity in the United States should be interpreted in light of the trauma of the Civil War.[14]

This list of examples could be extended endlessly to show the effects of the emotional reservoir of myth.

The above refers mainly to the national level, but there are other cases in which the ethos as well as the imprint from which it has emerged occur on a wider scale. For example, the Enlightenment, with its celebration of reason, liberty, and tolerance, took root in a long continental experience of superstition, dogmatism, and despotism, just as the cult of knowledge followed centuries of doctrinaire obscurantism. The same can be said of the relationship with nature in the West and elsewhere, a relationship of admiration, respect, and fear inspired both by its beauty and by its fearsome mood swings.[15]

The formation of the European Union, from the start, drew much from the ideals of peace, reconciliation, and cooperation, which themselves were responses to memories of the atrocities associated with the two world wars, despotisms, imperialisms, and genocides (directed against Jews and Roma).[16] These memories anchored the founding myth of the union. The message from all this has been expressed in two words: never again.

Again at the international level, Western imperialism on the Asian continent sowed the seeds for a negative anchor that is a source of resentment and even of a thirst for vengeance. However, according to P. Mishra (2012), prominent Asian intellectuals have difficulty giving shape to a coherent ethos on the basis of that painful imprint. Should Asia emulate the West according to an original Asian model? Should it project towards the future, towards the new horizons of globalization, in continuity with the restored ancient traditions? Or should it blend these two approaches?

In short, one could say that the goals and values upheld in the construction of the ethos correspond either (a) to those of which a society was sorely deprived during its history, or (b) to those with which it has been substantially endowed, or else (c) to those it failed to honour. But for the population to embrace them, these goals and values have to be forged in its past and maintain a strong resonance with it. I refer to the process by which a society builds an ethos from an imprint the "historicization" of values and ideals.[17]

The examples I have just given are quite predictable, but this is not always the case. For example, the (abortive) Jewish revolt led by Bar Kokhba against the Romans before the Christian era has been celebrated both as a painful defeat and as a victory (Y. Zerubavel, 2013). Similarly, according to R. Eyerman (2001), the experience of slavery among African Americans generated two opposing ethoses, one focusing on the continuous advancement of blacks, the other on the restoration of ancient pride. The Holocaust also inspired two different representations, one considered "progressive," the other "tragic" (J. C. Alexander, 2003, chapter 2). J. S. Bennett (2012) showed that the supposed appearances of the Virgin in Fatima in 1917 fuelled both a deeply conservative religious nationalism and an authoritarian republicanism. In France, the memory of the Second World War generated contradictory ethoses fuelled either by a feeling of shame because of submission to the Occupier, or by a feeling of pride related to acts of resistance (O. Wieviorka, 2012). In contrast, in societies such as Russia, Australia, English Canada, the United States, and Great Britain, a unanimously triumphant ethos prevailed.[18]

Finally, the founding myths and heroes of Quebec have inspired contradictory narratives that continue to divide the national imaginary and to inspire (or reflect) opposing political orientations. This is evident in disagreements surrounding the memory of the 1760 conquest, but also in more specific episodes that are just as controversial, such as the celebration in 1908 of the tercentenary of Quebec City as well as the commemoration of founding heroes such as Champlain and Bishop Laval (H. V. Nelles, 2003; R. Rudin, 2005).[19]

Note that an ethos, as a manifestation of values, beliefs, and aspirations, speaks to the future as much as to the present. It influences behaviours and indicates pathways for collective mobilization in the form of projects or utopias. We recognize in this the two faces of values, which are expressed both in a code of ethics in the strict sense (principles, norms) and in a teleology.

The construction of a myth, therefore, cannot be a one-way operation, initiated solely by the powers that be. For a message to become rooted deeply in the collective consciousness, it needs to be skilfully formulated and conveyed by influential actors, but it also has to resonate with a meaningful, emotional experience in the past of the target population.

Finally, even though it is always presented as an obvious corollary of the anchor and the imprint, the ethos is also clearly a matter of choice. This dimension is usually obscured, but it is sometimes laid bare. It can be seen clearly in the Declaration of Independence of the thirteen American colonies in 1776, which states (in its second paragraph): "We hold these truths to be self-evident, that all men are created equal, that they are endowed by their Creator with certain unalienable Rights," and so on. The statement suggests that other options could have been presented but that the drafters chose to rule them out.

E. Sacralization

Sacralization is the crucial stage in the formation of a social myth. It lies at the heart of what could be called its immune system; it is above all thanks to this attribute that myth can endure and survive opposition and contradictions. This is also the most complex and the most intriguing stage of the mythification process.

The Cognitive Shift

Essentially, this step is defined by a cognitive shift, such that emotion takes over from reason as the primary engine of consciousness. Through this transformation, which opens the way to sacredness, social myths transcend other collective representations, in particular the symbolic "resources" that make up "repertoires" (symbols, customs, traditions, models of behaviour, etc.).

Myths belong to what S. Moscovici (1984, pp. 9–14) calls "prescriptive representations." For example, could we say that a young black

South African "chooses" to endorse the ideal of racial equality? Does a US citizen really feel free to support the principle of civil liberties, the right of individual property, and democracy? Does the ideal of gender equality in the West belong to the options of a free market of ideas governed by reason? Each of these examples gives us a glimpse into the taboo aspect of myth and the power it gains from sacredness. They suggest that the deepest, largely unconscious foundations of identity and moral convictions through which each individual structures his or her life are not primarily the results of strategic, contextual choices. These convictions instead appear to be strongly oriented (if not in large part dictated) by the deep roots of the self, sustained by myth.[20] They also emerge from intense acculturation starting in early childhood.

The Conditions for the Cognitive Shift

With respect to the cognitive shift associated with sacralization, we need to examine the conditions that make it possible. At this stage in my study, I cannot yet provide a satisfactory answer to this question. But the action of a few factors can be clearly seen.

There is first of all the general human need for a corpus of basic meanings required for the construction of individual identities, especially the adoption of deep convictions, whether religious or other. Collectively, and this time from a Durkheimian perspective, this corpus of meanings will contribute to maintaining the social bond and ensuring the survival of the whole community.

Second, sacralization originates in the search – again characteristic of the human condition – for some form of transcendence, ideal, or absolute that can bring satisfaction in various ways: in religion per se (the supernatural), but also in philosophy, art, science, celebration of nature (in the manner of romantics or ecologists). Consider here also the search for love, the cult of the family or the nation, heroism, athletic feats, and so on. It is also understood that this quest can be motivated in various ways: by a need to allay fear, by a yearning for wonderment and enchantment, or by a desire to achieve a higher level of consciousness or existence that belongs to the sphere of the divine. More generally, transcendence fulfils the need to go beyond the limitations of daily life. This is the world of dream, of escape outside the immediate boundaries of existence.

By referring to the concept of transcendence, I am therefore adopting, within the non-rational, a very broad meaning of the sacred that covers its religious and secular dimensions, but without conflating them[21] and without establishing a hierarchy between them. In this regard, these two concepts of sacred and transcendence can be considered synonymous. One could say that the sacred (or transcendence), which flourishes in religion, is differentiated from non-religious forms in that the former usually involves a duality, a separation between a natural order and a supernatural order (animistic religions being the exception: religion is everywhere, and nature, so to speak, is nowhere). In the other paths to transcendence, continuity within the natural order is not really broken. Note also that the ambivalence – so often commented on – within the sacred between attraction and fear (R. Otto, 1968) is especially associated with the religious form. However, whether it is the sacred in the religious sense or in the secular sense, in both cases there is a cognitive shift from the intellect to the non-rational.[22]

Third, each generation is heir to a capital of greatness and heroism, but also of suffering and sacrifice (or martyrdom), that has been assembled in the course of the history of their society or in the past of their civilization. This capital, by highlighting the pursuit of the absolute, opens the way to transcendence. This symbolic heritage, embodied in memory, reinforces a moral sense focusing on honour and loyalty.

A fourth factor concerns the taboo aspect of myth. As mentioned above, myth conceals as much as it reveals. In every community there are troubling, shameful, or devastating truths that the members are loath to face and prefer to repress. This forms a wall of repulsion that fuels a kind of reverse sacralization.

The final factor is based on the aggressive vision of a Them–Us boundary sustained by a sense of peril or a desire for vengeance. The impact of this vision is all the stronger given that it is usually expressed through Manichean representations and polarizing arguments.

One might wonder if the cognitive shift is an individual phenomenon or a collective one. The most likely answer is that it straddles these two spheres. Like any collective representation, it is a social fact in the sense that it results from life in society and acts on it. But it is inconceivable that it does not deeply affect individual consciousness. Its features must therefore be sought in both directions.

Finally, as a component of mythification, sacralization substantially changes the status of the initial message, but it also operates on a set of symbols that contribute to the cognitive shift.

Strictly speaking, these first five elements of mythification belong to the genesis of social myth. The connections among them are both logical and sequential. By contrast, the next three elements operate in a rather transversal way in the mythification process, for they belong instead to a symbolic engineering focusing on acculturation and more precisely on the accreditation of the message. These are mechanisms that govern the path leading to sacralization.

F. The Narrative

This component consists primarily in the construction of a **narrative** supported by practices of commemoration. The goal of this is to activate the emotion associated with the anchor and the imprint in order to bolster the ethos.[23] Ritual plays a key role here. It translates abstract values into actual experiences, reinforced by dramatizations intended to create or intensify the sense of belonging. It also establishes or evokes symbols that embody these values, giving them concrete features; such symbols include notable sites, objects, or figures and triumphant or sacrificed heroes. Note that the construction of symbols leads to a parallel process analogous to that of mythification. This is, in fact, an old avenue of research, one that focuses more or less on the same questions: How do certain sites, objects, or figures embody in the eyes of a social group or society mythified values and beliefs? How is this kind of association perpetuated, and then broken to be replaced by another? Who are the promoters of these operations? And so on.

I use the concept of symbol in its most familiar meaning: a sign that is in itself arbitrary (an object, a place, one person, etc.) but that in a given context has come to be closely associated with a message. Another meaning, current in studies of the imaginary, makes the symbol a manifestation, a resonance of the unconscious or of an archetype; the relationship between the sign and the signified is therefore structural and permanent (the meaning of the circle, night, fire, etc.). Similarly, for others, the symbol provides access to the immanence of the sacred.

Finally, the narrative itself – or, more broadly, the construction of memory – uses various channels: iconography, historical scholarship, stories and legends, museums, the novel, the media, and historical re-enactments.

Activating the Anchor and the Imprint: Historicization of Values

When the memory of injuries or exploits fades, the myth loses its hold. This is why the construction, teaching, and dissemination of collective memory are always eminently political; all are sites of controversies and often of redefinitions conditioned by power relations.

Among many others, the case of Quebec, once again, is instructive in this regard. For the past few years, arguments around the teaching of national history have divided intellectuals, political parties, and public opinion. The most recent reform, implemented by the provincial Liberal government, was accused of overlooking founding events of the national imaginary, in particular the Conquest of 1760, which transformed New France into a British colony. In the eyes of many, this event is the main anchor of Quebec memory, the one that fuels the desire for collective emancipation and, especially, nationalist and sovereigntist aspirations (see G. Bouchard, 2013e).

The narrative brings to the fore the historicization of values that has taken place in the past of a society and that lies at the heart of its symbolic heritage. Historicization designates the process of appropriation through which a value permeates an imaginary. From this perspective, the past of any society can be viewed as a reservoir of defining experiences (positive or negative) from which are forged sensibilities, aspirations, and ideals. However, this is the result of constant work of interpretation, selection, and promotion. Selection is a key step since the values in a society's past are not all commendable.[24] By virtue of these operations, a value forged within a particular history can gradually acquire a civic, universalizing scope and thus assume another existence. Accordingly, thanks to historicization, the symbolic content carried by the mythification process enjoys increased legitimacy and influence.

A prime example, already mentioned, of the process of historicization is provided by the value of gender equality in Quebec. Its growth is born out of a combination of factors, such as the struggles by women's groups and the pursuit of a universal ideal strongly activated at the international level beginning in the mid-twentieth century. But the particular experience of women in Quebec's past (marked by the forms of oppression practised by the Catholic clergy) also weighed heavily. Like many others, this example shows how a combination of reason and emotion harnessed by a narrative led to the emergence of a value of universal scope and became an engine for a vigorous social movement.

Identical values, universal in nature, are cultivated in many countries, but in the course of historicization they acquire a distinctive resonance. For example, the value of equality takes on very different accents in the contexts of Norway (equality of conditions and living standards),

France (equality of citizen's rights), and the United States (equality of opportunity). The same is true for the values of freedom, democracy, social justice, and the like. Thanks to the process of appropriation inherent in historicization, universal and potentially abstract values thereby acquire specific, familiar faces.

Healing or Reopening Wounds?

Practices of commemoration often seek to mitigate and overcome the effect of a traumatic experience.[25] But at other times, their aim is the opposite. Instead of being a process of healing, they are a means of periodically reopening the wound in order to reawaken and perpetuate it, of reviving the myth by re-energizing it. For this purpose, powerful images such as sacrifice, solidarity, heroism, and the duty of loyalty to worthy predecessors are commonly used. A similar logic motivates the remembrance of major exploits, which are thus given a new life.

On this point, I differ from the assertions of H. White (1999), who finds only debilitating effects in practices of commemoration when they are not intended to heal the wound. I think on the contrary that they can often support dreams of collective emancipation, as shown by the example of societies that have lived for a long time under the yoke of colonization or despotism. The Quebec poet Gaston Miron showed that the experience of collective suffering can be open to a universal solidarity (see, for example, his poem "L'Octobre" in *L'Homme rapaillé* (The Reconstructed Man), in which he invites us to "tie our roots of suffering to the universal pain within each repressed man").

Likewise, it is clear that in communist regimes established by revolution, the constant reminders of capitalist crimes did *not* have healing or amnesia as a goal. Nor is it certain that the many commemorations of the Shoah have the objective of easing the pain. Rather, it seems that their purpose is to constantly rekindle the flame of humanism through contact with a traumatic memory. In this same vein, almost all of the former Soviet republics liberated by the fall of the Iron Curtain have built museums to preserve the memory of the horrors of despotism (in Hungary there is even a "House of Terror"). We also know that nations often perpetuate the memory of past sacrifices and defeats in order to strengthen collective identity or inspire a desire for reconquest.

Here, the case of Bolivia is particularly enlightening. In the aftermath of a war against Chile in the late nineteenth century, that country lost its access to the ocean. It has nevertheless maintained a national navy (without a fleet), and it has established 23 March of each year as a day of mourning to remember that amputation and to nurture dreams of recovering its seacoast (L. Perrier-Bruslé, 2011, 2013).

We see here how the use of the memory of traumatic events to support mythification differs from the approach taken by psychoanalysis. In the latter case, the original wound is often repressed by the individual as a means of defence, which leads to various pathogenic effects (including neuroses). The work of the therapist consists therefore in bringing this wound to consciousness in order to heal or deactivate it.[26] In the case of social myth, quite the contrary, commemoration has above all the effect of poking the wound in order to perpetuate it.[27] This being said, an analogy remains with the psychoanalytic mechanisms, given that the narrative that awakens the wound also consigns to oblivion certain aspects of the anchor that feeds the taboo.

Finally, following the logic of the scapegoat (see S. J. Mock (2012a), commemoration is meant to absolve the guilt felt by the members of the nation who have committed the sacrificial act by expunging the golden age. However, this hypothesis is worth verifying empirically.[28]

The Immunity of Myth

We can thus better understand the authority enjoyed by myth. Based only partly on rationality, it is largely immunized against critical arguments or counter-proposals. To attack myth, to call it into question, is to deny the emotions and suffering it embodies; it is to impugn the greatness of past acts, the honour of sacrificed heroes; it is also to destroy the pride, fascination, and elements of transcendence that nourish the mind. Similarly, exposing repressed taboos undermines the good conscience of a community. So it is hardly surprising that the reaction to this kind of criticism is often emotional, even aggressive.

In fact, this whole dynamic does not belong to the realm of reason or argument, but to the realm of healing (in the case of negative anchors and imprints), or of enchantment and loyalty (in the case of anchors and imprints fuelled by triumphant references), or else of concealment (in the case of taboo). One way or another, the powerful prohibitions that weigh on the message and that are revealed when it is opposed confirm that it is indeed imbued with sacredness.

In light of the above, recall that the narrative and the various forms of commemoration are indispensable to mythification, but again, that does not turn myth into narrative, as claimed by many authors. Myth remains basically a sacralized representation of values and beliefs that is rooted in memory because it was forged in a history.

The Role of Rituals

Commemoration often involves ritual. This symbolic practice has been the subject of many analyses in numerous societies and has been given many definitions. Some authors have posited that rituals retell the act of the creation of the world or establish a mediation with the divine. But many other functions have been assigned to them: to reduce anxiety about the unknown (Malinowski, Victor Turner, and others), to sustain identity, to maintain social bonds and balance (Durkheim, Victor Turner), to divert the threat of violence to a victim (René Girard), to atone for a transgression (Freud), to place someone in a social hierarchy (Bourdieu), to restore the continuity of experience that myth sometimes has failed to secure (Lévi-Strauss).

But for the purposes of commemoration and mythification, the elements of ritual that seem to be the most important are these: (a) the celebration of the meaning of the initial message based on a remembrance and sometimes on a reconstitution of the anchor, (b) the interaction (intersubjectivity) that favours performance among the actors and the identification that results from it, (c) the emotion produced by the performance, and (d) the feeling of unity and even of solidarity that motivates the actors. The lives of nations offer the best examples of these kinds of rituals, whether these are traditional national festivities or episodes that showcase the nation – for example, the Olympic Games.[29]

Osmosis of Anchors and Imprints

Finally, on a more technical level, many authors have discussed the relationship between anchor and narrative. According to one thesis, this relationship is not monolithic. M. Rothberg (2009), for example, introduced the concept of multidirectional memory to establish the idea that different anchors (in this case, the experiences of the Holocaust and colonization) could cross-fertilize. The author shows that the narratives of colonization prepared the way for the memory of the Holocaust by nourishing a sensitivity to human dignity and human rights. Bridges and points of convergence can thus be established between different anchors, galvanizing the ethos and the narrative that are associated with them.

Going further, J. C. Alexander (2004) suggests that various groups can come to share anchors associated with the same traumatic events. This seems very likely, given, for example, the humanitarian dimension building on genocides and racisms. Also, migrants can share feelings inspired by a noteworthy event in the past of their adopted society.

Finally, according to an analogous but inverse logic, a single anchor can sometimes sustain different founding myths. This is the case with the poem "Évangéline" by Longfellow, which gave rise to three founding myths (Acadian, American, and Louisianan) (J.-Y. Thériault, 2013).[30]

G. Techniques of Persuasion

Obeying the same logic as narratives, techniques of persuasion are aimed at formulating or reformulating the central message of the myth according to changing challenges, publics, and contexts. They are also aimed at disseminating and instilling the message in the population. These processes of persuasion, active in all the components examined so far, use a wide range of channels of communication, from politics and social sciences to literature and the arts. They operate mainly in the following six areas:

1. **Visualization**, namely, the use of images (photos, drawings, caricatures, etc.) that summarize and accentuate the message's meaning. The decisive role of visualization was demonstrated brilliantly by G. Zubrzycki (2013b) in his study of the Saint-Jean-Baptiste parades in Quebec during the 1960s. Contemporary eco-myth also favours visual media to illustrate environmental damage and the urgency to act on it; the polar bear, an innocent victim trapped on its ice floe, has become, along with dolphins and baby seals, a universal symbol.

2. **Rhetoric**, understood here in a limited sense. It includes stylistic and visual effects, allegories, antitheses, hyperbole, tropes, gestures, and so on. It also includes stratagems such as omission, blanket generalizations, understatement, and exaggeration. This dimension should not be underestimated. It played a key role in government in ancient Greek and Roman cities. Closer to our time, consider Lincoln's Gettysburg Address of 1863 and Martin Luther King's "I have a dream..." speech in Washington a century later. In short, the power of oratory has been a reality in all eras.

3. **Figurations**, in the sense of the creation of discursive figures, with their arrangements and their enunciative inventions. Figuration goes beyond rhetorical devices per se by mobilizing keywords, ideas, and strong images that are deeply rooted in the collective imaginary and that play on archetypes, ensuring them a strong resonance with the audience. Two forms can be distinguished. *Microfigures* are simple formulations, sometimes just a few words that make a catchy expression. In Quebec, at the most elementary level, one thinks of clichés such as "drawers of water," "white niggers," "born for a small crust of bread," "having the wool sheared off our backs," "masters in our own house," "the Saint-Jean sheep," "stand up for ourselves," "a tiny drop in an English-speaking sea" (to illustrate the fragility of French-speaking Quebec in America).

The "bas de laine" ("wool sock," meaning "nest egg") is another loaded term, coming from the period when French Canadians, many living in poverty at the bottom of the social ladder in Canada, jealously hoarded in a wool sock the little money they had managed to save. Many were living in poverty and were reluctant to entrust their precious savings to banks. To this day, people talk about the "bas de laine des Québécois" to refer to the Caisse de dépôt et placement, which manages the Quebec pension fund.

Microfigures are the equivalent of the "frame," a common concept in American sociology. In its current usage, "framing" refers to techniques for formulating a message that encourage certain interpretations and discourage others. This process consists in encoding, condensing, and simplifying.[31] It is aimed at establishing the best match possible between, on the one hand, the form and content of the message, and on the other, the expectations, sensibilities, and allegiances of the target population.[32]

Precise rules determine the effectiveness of the microfiguration: descriptions of situations must be concise and easily understood, the contexts are presented as likely to be changed through the will of the actors, the Them–Us polarity should be very explicit, the statement of ideas or questions favours binary forms, the adversary is never an abstract force (such as the evolution of the market or globalization) but rather a set of clearly identified individuals, the argument appeals to familiar narratives and characters and to broadly internalized norms, the position of the adversary is associated with disagreeable images, and so on.

Politics and advertising are the sites of microfiguration par excellence. For example, in the United States, the majority of wealthy Republicans react rather badly to government programs intended to reduce inequalities; for them, the very idea goes against the American Dream by suggesting that it is immoral to get rich. By contrast, fighting poverty gives rise to a more positive reaction (or a less negative one) to the extent that it emphasizes patronage, the morality and generosity of the rich. In the same sense, the plan for assistance to families initiated by Richard Nixon in 1968 was very favourably welcomed, unlike the minimum guaranteed income proposed by presidential candidate George McGovern in 1972. That election plank, designed to help less fortunate individuals, was also seen as contrary to the American Dream, which views every individual as responsible for his or her own social destiny. In a related sphere, we are also aware of how much in the past few years the expression Main Street/Wall Street has become popular.

In the field of advertising, microfiguration sometimes uses unexpected tricks. For example, the slogan "clean coal," introduced in 2012 in the United States, is a blatant oxymoron; but that was precisely the intention. Rather than try to hide the most obvious negative aspects of the coal industry and thus make a kind of admission, the plan was to blatantly deny the negatives by celebrating their opposites. Sometimes the ruse is more transparent but no less effective. An example is the policy introduced during Bill Clinton's first term that sentenced criminals to life imprisonment after a third felony conviction. The initiative was called "Three Strikes and You're Out!" The clever reference to the most elementary – and least contentious – rule in baseball was used instead of any real argument.[33]

As for meta-figures, these are more elaborate argumentative constructs that involve a set of microfigures and can be likened to interpretative charts. They correspond quite closely to the concept of "master frame" proposed by D. A. Snow & R. D. Benford (1992). Here are some examples, taken once again from Quebec history: the discourse of conquest and reconquest (see below), as well as those of revenge of the cradle, survival, the *Grande Noirceur* (Great Darkness), and Americanity.

Finally, the logic of microfigures and meta-figures can also be applied to literary studies. For example, it has been demonstrated that the theme of garbage (or remains), combined with a discourse of disenchantment and parody, constitutes the matrix of the work of Réjean Ducharme (É. Nardout-Lafarge, 2001). According to M. Biron (2000), the stories of Jacques Ferron are structured around the idea of liberty (capacity to reinvent one's life, to start again). Similarly, the symbolism of the moon is said to be key to the novels of Michel Tremblay (A. Brochu, 2002),[34] while the work of Dany Laferrière is said to revolve around the image of drifting, and so on.[35]

4. **Argumentative mechanisms**. These are discursive procedures that govern the construction of ideologies. Here are a few examples:

a) *Recycling.* This mechanism consists in adopting the structure and vocabulary of an ideology that is well established in a society and then shifting its meaning by imperceptibly inserting additional content in order to use it for other purposes.

Relying on syncretism, this technique operates through shifts in words and meaning, while avoiding disturbing the structure of the established imaginary in order to benefit from the energy it produces. Recycling can involve songs, poems, and films as well as historiographical narratives or political ideologies.

The process was very well illustrated by J. Prokop (1995), who showed how, after 1945, the Soviets attempted to reclaim old Polish founding myths and transform them into vectors of communism, hoping to inspire a sense of belonging to the Soviet ideology. For example, Germany, which had often humiliated Poland in the name of its racial superiority, remained the enemy, but now it was made to embody the most hateful features of capitalism. An analogous scenario unfolded during the same period in Romania (I. Buşe, 2008, pp. 136–138).

In the same vein, K. Hayward (2009) has shown how, in Ireland, the political elites subtly adjusted the old nationalist discourse so as to open it to the idea of the European Union. In Israel, popular songs about globalization have been reworked so that they can serve the national cause (G. Hermoni & U. Lebel, 2013). Following the same logic, the theorists of Aryanism in the nineteenth century camouflaged their argument under the guise of Darwinism. At the same time, the nation took the place of nobility as the seat of the superior race (H. Tudor, 1972).[36]

Another form of recycling occurs when, without altering the discourse, the symbolic impetus of a myth and the energy it produces are used for purposes other than the original one. This was the case in Quebec in 2013–14 during the debate around the Quebec Charter of Values, proposed by the Parti québécois government in Bill 60.

The charter, which proposed restricting freedom of religion by pro-hibiting the wearing of religious symbols by public and parapublic employees, clearly affected immigrants and members of ethnocul-tural minorities (mainly Jews, Muslims, and Sikhs). It also had the goal of protecting the identity of the francophone majority, which was said to be threatened by values and beliefs associated with reli-gious minorities.

To mobilize the members of the majority in favour of the bill, the gov-ernment spokesperson called on them to "stand up for themselves" or to "put on their pants" (pull up their socks), according to the expression favoured by the minister responsible, Bernard Drainville). In Quebec, these formulas traditionally refer to a powerful myth in the national imaginary, reminding francophones that they have a duty to stand up to all the forms of dependence (colonial and others) from which their society has suffered since the British Conquest of 1760. The myth was now being used against a new "enemy," but it was no longer the powerful or the colonizers who were being targeted; instead, it was the most vulnerable elements of society.

b) *Diversion*. In countries that have been struck by domestic acts of violence in reaction to a long tradition of discriminatory policies, official discourse speaks readily, not of the wrongdoings committed by those countries, but of crimes against humanity. This is a way to absolve oneself of any fault and to avoid any critical examination by diverting attention. Blaming the persistence of serious social pathologies on the weaknesses of human nature can be an effective way to mask government inaction.

c) *Contamination*. This process consists in discrediting a proposal or an ideology by likening it to a unanimously dismissed thesis. In the West, saying that the discourse of an enemy smacks of fascism or racism tends to weaken or neutralize it.

d) *Polarization*. This consists in defusing counter-arguments and explaining away recalcitrant data by casting them as belonging to one end of a dichotomy, preferably constructed on a moralistic axis. One example is the axis of evil that was invoked by President George W. Bush after the 11 September attacks in order to justify the invasion of Iraq and then the occupation of Afghanistan. Another is the polarities underlying Marxist theory (lords/vassals, bourgeois/proletarians, exploiters/exploited). The dramatization of issues, thereby distracting others from their empirical reality, also belongs to polarization.

e) *Conflation.* Artificially connecting a series of arguments by distorting reality.

f) *Conspiracy theories.* Playing on fear, such theories usually consist in setting a population against an imaginary enemy who is said to be deviously active inside or just outside its boundaries. Their aim is to discredit a group or a whole nation and to justify discriminatory measures. This process draws much of its effectiveness from the fact that it is extremely difficult to prove the non-existence of a conspiracy, since conspiracies, by their very nature, are not visible.

g) *Scapegoating.* For a society, this consists in arbitrarily assigning to an individual or group responsibility for a misfortune or offence by making that individual or group an expiatory victim.[37]

h) *Domino theory.* This is used to give credence to an attitude or a policy that is in itself unjustifiable, by assuming that if we allow A, then we will have to agree to B then C, and who knows to what extremes this will lead us? This process is often used in various Western societies in the current debate on secularism. For example, if the government accepts the wearing of religious signs in a specific circumstance, how can it prohibit them in any other situations? And if the wearing of religious symbols is permitted, what other concessions will it be forced to accept? The same process can be used to justify an initiative aimed at preserving a position or an advantage: if we do not protect A, we will have to sacrifice B, then everything else.

i) *Trojan Horse.* This mechanism is analogous to the previous one. It consists in making a harmless episode the prelude to a catastrophic scenario. In a spirit of prevention, wisdom therefore tells us to immediately exercise vigorous repression, thus preventing the dreaded scenario from coming to fruition.

These devices, and similar ones, inspire statements that can be true or simply be lies. In any case, they are powerfully persuasive. By establishing a clear cohesiveness, accessible to everyone, they describe reality in simple terms using a reasonable explanation. Also, some of them make it possible to anticipate future developments and to protect against their deleterious effects.

5. **Forms or structures of thought.** Any ideology – and more generally, any discursive construct intended to propose a vision of society – is immediately faced with contradictions in the form of

dichotomies. One way or another, it has to combine imperatives, values, and ideals that are socially attractive and legitimate but that in reality are in competition. This is the case, for example, with freedom and equality, tradition and change, the national and the social, the individual and the community, unity and diversity, the specific and the universal. An immense theoretical horizon opens up here, given the omnipresence or universality of contradiction, as Hegel and Marx have shown (G. Bouchard, 2003a, pp. 31–36).

More specifically, a contradiction can be overcome using discursive tricks, but it can also compromise the development of an intellectual framework, and it can even affect a society's course. During the first decades of the twentieth century, the project of national liberation of Quebecers put forward by the conservative elites collided with a general suspicion of the state. But how was it possible to work effectively for the emancipation of the nation without using the political sphere? This position led inevitably to a dead end. The situation in which many Indigenous populations in Quebec find themselves presents the same kind of difficulty: How do you modernize community life and open broader horizons for the young generation without sacrificing traditional culture, especially in its essential relationship with ancestral territory? In other words, how is one to avoid, on the one hand, turning inward and stagnation, and on the other hand, disruption and assimilation?

On another level, how can one maintain the model of the nation (with its premises of homogeneity and unity) in societies characterized by ethnocultural diversity? Or how can one create a feeling of solidarity where divisions, conflicts, and relationships of domination are rampant?

It is the work of reason to find ways out of the dead ends of collective life and, more generally, to establish cohesiveness or an appearance of cohesiveness in the disorder of social reality and in the lines of tension underlying it. Various strategies can be used, but, directly or not, they always rely on myths, which inform social thought. Myths help reason establish a cohesiveness and effectiveness in thought. But their contribution goes much further than this: they provide the non-rational side that the systems of thought need in order to incite the masses to act. Because in social matters – this is one of the themes of this book – reason alone is not enough to create an enduring sense of belonging and deep motivations.

I thus construe social thought as both positive and dynamic – that is, as a rational construction that is supported and propelled by myth and that is designed to (a) take into account the situation and the movement of a society (positive dimension) and (b) drive it in a given direction (dynamic dimension). Ideology, then, is the product of social thought and a combination of reason and myth.

I therefore address social thought from the angle of contradiction and look for ways to overcome the dichotomies it creates. From this perspective, one can distinguish, first of all, a form of **linear** or **radical** thought. Favouring maximum cohesiveness, it suppresses contradiction by giving priority to one of the two opposing elements, thus sacrificing the other. This type of thought, in general, is aimed at establishing unity, symmetry, and uniformity. For example, Bolshevism suppresses freedom in favour of equality, and it subordinates the individual to society in the name of the revolution. Fascism also reduces freedom, and it bases the authoritarianism of the state on the ideal of the moral purity to be restored. The Republican regime established with the French Revolution sacrificed diversity to unity and ethnicity to citizenship in the name of equality of rights.

Radical thought accepts the most diverse ideologies, both left and right, progressive as well as reactionary. Yet sometimes, instead of dismissing one of the two contradictory terms, it places them in a hierarchy.

Median thought (or oblique thought, to borrow an expression from Octavio Paz), by contrast, refrains from exclusion or hierarchy. Working in the in-between, outside binary logic, it retains the two contradictory elements and seeks to link them by introducing a third element that performs a mediation (or triangulation). I call this form of thought **organic** since, like a catalyst, it manages to establish a cohesiveness and a creative tension, a source of energy, within the contradictory. As pointed out by S. Lupasco (1982), this tension is, however, never conclusively overcome, because the two terms of the contradiction remain. Organic thought therefore creates a relationship that forever must be adjusted and, if necessary, redefined.

For example, the myth of the American Dream, coupled with a very strong sense of individual responsibility, is capable of superseding the American egalitarian ideal in the name of freedom. At the same time, it helps preserve the social order by attributing inequalities to the responsibility of individuals (inequality of talents, efforts) rather than to an unfair social structure. It thus establishes the moral legitimacy of unlimited enrichment, which becomes not only tolerable but also desirable for the society. Freedom is thus reconciled with equality. It is the individual, and not society, that bears the burden of the system's failures and deficiencies.

Racial democracy in Brazil is another example of organic thought. Based on the myth of racial equality (between the Indigenous populations, the descendants of Europeans, and the descendants of African slaves), it maintains that economic and social inequalities are not of racial origin – even though this credo is contradicted by the empirical data. The history of ideas in the West is teeming with examples of this kind. Again I call this structure of thought organic because of its flexibility and its capacity for adaptation and renegotiation, as well as its pragmatism. It also has the power to contain forces of division by diverting them towards attitudes and behaviours of conciliation.[38]

Median thought can be characterized as **fragmentary** when it fails to establish a cohesiveness and a creative tension. The result is a heterogeneous juxtaposition of incompatible propositions or ideological segments. This form of thought tends to produce uncertainty, apathy, and stagnation (conversely, it can also be the reflection or effects of these features when they are structural). I have given striking examples of this thought in the history of ideas in French Canada (G. Bouchard, 2003b, 2004b).

Recentred thought challenges the postulate that forms the basis for dichotomy by rejecting the two terms and replacing them with another, more malleable equation. It can be dialectic, with the two terms of the dichotomy evolving towards a third term that merges and erases them. This is the model of the Hegelian or Marxist dialectic.

Here is one example taken from the history of the New World. The European colonizers considered themselves civilized, while the inhabitants of the colonies (Amerindians or Creoles) were seen as barbarians or degenerates. A counter-discourse took shape among the creole elites, according to whom (a) the Europeans were not as civilized as they claimed to be, (b) the New World was the heir to great Amerindian civilizations, certainly as advanced as those of the Europeans, and (c) the mixing of cultures in the New World, benefiting from the European and Amerindian heritages, would give birth to a new civilization the like of which had never existed in history. Thanks to this discourse, the terms of the initial dichotomy were set aside in favour of a third that transcended them. Readers will note the difference between this and organic thought, in which the two terms of the antinomy remain.

Similarly, the Martiniquan A. Césaire (1950) rejected the concept of negritude, the vehicle of a black/white dichotomy, in favour of a different proposition that highlighted in both groups a universal dimension, a shared aspiration for humanism. More generally, postcolonial thought has the characteristic of challenging any form of binary thought, which is accused of establishing a hierarchy in favour of European colonizers. Such forms include the centre/periphery, civilization/barbarism, purity/impurity, identity/otherness, and universality/provincialism polarities.

Here is another example: in the face of two goals of the nation considered to be incompatible (i.e., as combining specific characteristics with universalism), one will quite simply choose to dismiss the national framework and opt for a postnational logic. Likewise, the proposition that a colonized society should resort to revolution can clash with the ideal of non-violence. A recentred thought will therefore emphasize that, in reality, this society is not colonized or that it is possible to carry out a non-violent revolution. Again, the dichotomy is destroyed.

Recentred thought can also be baroque. Here, quite paradoxically, reason uses a non-Cartesian logic calling on the fantastic, the supernatural, the wonderful, or the magical. This form of thought is active mainly among Latin American intellectuals such as Gabriel García Marquez, Jorge Luis Borges, Pablo Neruda, Carlos Fuentes, and many others. In magic realism in particular, reason remains at the helm, but it allows itself a little mischief; it is eclectic, proliferating. On the whole, recentred thought has allowed the elites of the New World to call into question and reject the dichotomies that were imposed on them by European intellectuals and that placed them in positions of inferiority.

Finally, **parallel** thought does not seek to remedy the antinomy. Rather, it establishes a permanent face-to-face with the contradictory. But this strategy can be experienced in various ways. We can thus distinguish here nihilist, stoic, tragic, and ironic thought, and so forth. In each case, some motivation leads either to the abdication of reason, to an admission that one is incapable of expunging the contradictory, or to a renunciation resulting from a choice that can be motivated and shaped in various ways.

The contexts associated with parallel thought are variegated. It can be a society that has for a long time struggled in vain to free itself from oppression and that finally capitulated, giving in to the idea that it is impossible to change its destiny. It can be the result of an era of confusion, apathy, or indifference that feeds a feeling of powerlessness. It can be a powerful current of thought that emphasizes the figures of the absurd. In philosophy, this is the case with the pessimistic

German tradition (Schopenhauer,[39] Nietzsche, Kafka, etc.), the absurdist thinkers (Camus), the disenchanted playwrights and writers (Ionesco, Beckett, Céline, Cioran), and the Buddhist nirvana as absolute detachment. Finally, a remarkable illustration is Greek theatre (Sophocles, Aeschylus, Euripides), which features man as responsible for his acts and their consequences, but at the same time as a plaything of the gods, left to a fate that they impose on him arbitrarily.

This effort at classifying the structures of thought, although related to a different approach and a different goal, belongs to the logic illustrated by Ernst Cassirer (mythical thought), Claude Lévi-Strauss (the savage mind), Serge Gruzinski (the mestizo mind), Leon Festinger (cognitive dissonances and the three ways to reduce them – see L. Festinger, 1965; L. Festinger & A. Aronson, 1965), and a few others.[40]

The typology I am proposing is unique given that it helps to highlight the role of myth in the operations of reason, in particular to bolster radical thought or modes of mediation between two incompatible terms – since another of its functions consists in transcending contradictions. The typology is also a way to tackle a complex dimension, one that is difficult to measure but nevertheless essential – the dimension of symbolic effectiveness. Thought can affect the behaviour of individuals and social movements under certain conditions that have not been fully explored. This study is risky, but it should be possible to make some inroads. It would, however, be a bad idea to create a hierarchy of types of thought solely on the basis of their intrinsic effectiveness; the nature of contexts is another factor that weighs heavily.

The typology draws attention to significant structural characteristics and unprecedented recurrences within discursive strategies. We are here at a level of analysis that is much deeper than figuration or argumentative mechanisms, hence the relevance of this line of research.

Finally, this typology is based on a specific view of the role of reason in the operations of thought. Reason is usually perceived in its relationship with reality, which brings us to ponder its conformity to reality or truth. I am proposing instead that we consider reason in its relationship to myth and raise the question of its effectiveness – more precisely, of its capacity to overcome contradiction. In this respect, my approach is close to that of Claude Lévi-Strauss. According to Lévi-Strauss, however, this is the essential function of myth: to establish a mediation designed to overcome a binary opposition, to break a symbolic stalemate.[41] I believe I have shown that social myths fulfil other functions that are just as essential.

6. **Repertoires of discursive patterns.** Faced with a contradiction or a dead end, reason tries to restore cohesiveness by constructing bypasses. We discover, however, that for a given stalemate, there is not an unlimited number of possible solutions. The recurrences manifested in them bring us to the concept of repertoire. In this vein, we are already familiar with the social repertoires (or modes of collective action) analysed by C. Tilly (1995, 2006). Studying acts of social protest in the eighteenth and nineteenth centuries in France and in England, Tilly observed that subversive behaviours or grassroots movements can be reduced to a relatively limited register of forms of action. He found the cause in macrosocial factors – essentially the social regime characteristic of a given nation. Such a regime tolerates or favours certain forms of protest and creates obstacles to others.

M. Lamont & L. Thévenot (2000) have also analysed what they call national repertoires, as symbolic patterns to which the members of a disadvantaged and marginalized class or group can refer in order to define and valorize their identity (to restore a sense of dignity) as well as their place in society. The authors have shown how these criteria differ between France and the United States. In the first case, principles of social solidarity (equality, human dignity, universality of rights) are often mentioned; in the latter case, references to the market (norms of consumption and wealth) are very frequent.[42]

The concept of discursive repertoires seems quite close to what M. Angenot (1988) calls "topical repertoires" (p. 83 ff.). However, his concept of a "global regulatory system" is instead related to my concept of master myth or archemyth (see chapter 5), even though I am somewhat reluctant to accept the idea of a totalizing or hegemonic culture. Collective imaginaries are hard to reduce to such a restrictive geometry.

The discursive repertoires I want to emphasize here are composed of more or less effective schemas (or recurring configurations) that give substance to the concept of a grammar of thought – or at least to certain of its operations.[43] Here are a few examples from the history of the nations of the New World.

Paradoxically, the new nations were seeking to establish a long memory that would situate their origins in distant times. The goal was to provide the emergent, fragile, often challenged nation with symbolic substance and greater moral authority. The various formulas developed fell under three strategies: to define oneself in continuity with the European mother country by claiming its distant, prestigious roots; to identify with the Native population (Incas, Mayas, Aztecs, etc.) and appropriate their ancient past along with their remarkable heritage; or to turn to popular culture, represented either as a timeless corpus of stories, traditions, and languages, or as the vehicle of an original culture formed since the settling of the New World. In two or three cases only (including the United States), new nations have opted to dispense with long-term memory and to project themselves into the future, feeding on the symbolism of their founding act.

New nations have had to overcome another roadblock: the diversity of their populations (made up of Creoles, Amerindians, and often blacks) impeded the establishment of the national model borrowed from Europe, which postulated ethnocultural homogeneity. The principal solutions adopted have borrowed the following approaches: to build on a common denominator beyond the differences (the territory, for example, or fundamental values); to declare that the heterogeneous segments originate from a single, very old stock (biological, religious, linguistic, etc.), thus establishing the basis for kinship and community; or to affirm that the differences are disappearing as a result of intense mixing.

Another example of the problems faced by the New World's elites: as they experienced strong feelings of inferiority in the face of the cultural richness of the European countries, they sought to erase the image of their mediocrity and, at the same time, to overcome the contemptuous discourse to which they were being subjected by many European intellectuals (a state of savagery, a return to animality, etc.). For this purpose, five approaches were often taken:

a) *Piracy.* This approach was practised in many settler societies, which, to free themselves from cultural dependence on Europeans, chose to steal or pirate their symbols (language, religion, customs). These symbols thus became spoils of war.[44]

b) *Cannibalism.* According to a cannibal metaphor that first appeared in Brazil, the descendants of Europeans appropriated the metropolitan culture by devouring it. They then fed on its virtues and, to affirm their independence, turned them against the Europeans. This interpretation was also a reference to Brazil's indigenous people, who were thereby accorded a kind of recognition.

c) *Profanation.* This pattern of thought consisted of parodying (even "violating") the culture of the mother country by targeting its greatest masterpieces. By disrupting and inverting the norms of the beautiful and the true, the colonial elites sabotaged the cultural authority of the metropolis and freed themselves from a humiliating, burdensome authority.

d) *Bastardy.* According to this metaphor, the degree zero of the culture was decreed by dismissing all European heritages. The next stage was to then readmit parts of those cultures, but freely, as if by choice. This was another appropriation mechanism.

e) *Takeover of civilization.* A common vision affirmed that the Old World was in decline and that the nations of the New World were going to soon take over from Western civilization. This pattern is close to the strategy of inversion, according to which the cultures of the New World are viewed as intrinsically superior because of the vitality arising from their youth on an untamed territory.[45]

National myths are another site of repertoires. Since time immemorial, in every country, the dominant elites have set out to establish the nation on a symbolic foundation in order to ensure the perpetuation of their power and to secure the endorsement of that power by the population. Thus, from one place or one century to another, the nation has been defined as a family; as a living organism all of whose parts should come together; as a creation of God (the head of the nation thus becoming His emissary or His descendant); as a people vested with a divine mission; as occupying the centre of the planet, from which it spreads to all other nations; as transcendent because of the purity and superiority of its race; as the vehicle of a particular genius that makes it exceptional; or as threatened by enemies. Finally, at the same time, the working classes and sometimes the peasants have sometimes been designated as forming the heart of the nation.

As noted earlier, many nations, in order to give meaning to their past and to their present, have also used some variant of the millenarian model, according to which the nation had once known happier times, which were interrupted by a great misfortune that plunged it into decline, which has ushered in an era of struggle, of reconquest, to repair the wound and re-establish the initial state of happiness.[46]

Beyond their intrinsic interest as discursive strategies, knowledge of these mechanisms, repertoires, and structures of thought is useful for a better understanding of ideologies and public debate. Such knowledge also makes it easier to deconstruct these strategies to test their validity and to bring out what they may conceal, given that they often constitute claims that serve some power. This is what, among other things, A. O. Hirschman (1991) taught us with his repertoire of the three possible arguments that can be made against proposed changes. The first denounces the negative effects of the plan (it will make the situation worse); the second is aimed at its futility (the plan will change nothing); the third views the costs of the proposed change as excessive, given the doubtful projected effects (the remedy is worse than the illness).

Returning to dissemination and techniques of persuasion, we observe that social actors resort to a multitude of channels. Some of the principal channels are television and literature (especially popular novels), the school system, the social and historical sciences, popular rituals, cinema, political discourse, and iconography – to which we can now add social networks. As for the media, they have always been called upon; we know that B. Anderson (1983) saw them as the ideal instrument for disseminating national sentiment.

Some of the characteristic experiences of dissemination and accreditation are related to the construction of national myths and national identities in the nineteenth and twentieth centuries. Among many possible examples, let us mention the role assigned in France to the school and the army in the dissemination of the Republican myth (thoroughly studied in the many works of Maurice Agulhon); the very effective propaganda of the Mexican government starting in the nineteenth century using the media and the schools (N. Guttiérez, 1999); the construction of the Finnish identity using popular novels, satirical magazines, and postcards, and even the contribution of the scout movement there (D. Fewster, 2006); the use of museums by the Bolsheviks to build a Soviet culture (F. Hirsh, 2005); the cultural offensive carried out in the 1930s by the Second Spanish Republic in order to instil in the population a modern nationality that was both Castilian and open to Europe, which made intensive use of film and popular theatre to overcome widespread illiteracy, especially in the countryside (S. Holguin, 2002); and, finally, the wide-ranging activities orchestrated by the Canadian government in recent decades to establish multiculturalism as a national myth.

There are also transnational examples of dissemination and accreditation. For example, P. Levitt and S. Merry (2009) were able to delineate the complex process of the establishment of women's rights in four countries (China, Peru, India, and the United States). Their study highlights the diversity of the strategies used and how the central message was adapted to the specific contextual characteristics to ensure that it was easily accessible and meaningful for the target audiences (the authors speak of a process of "vernacularization"). Close attention was also paid to choices of symbols, heroines, and narratives. The result has been a great diversity of means in the service of a single crucial idea.

On the margins of the mythification process, one can be attracted by the idea of differentiating stages in the dissemination and accreditation of a message, in a journey from initial statement to sacralization. Strong efforts to that end have been made in the communication sciences. The message thus goes through a series of steps defined in terms of the type of endorsement (more or less rational), the type of hold on individual minds, and the degree of internalization. In this vein, researchers have conceived a sequence of stages as follows: (a) information, (b) opinion, (c) conviction, (d) belief, and so on. We can also imagine a sequence based on the type or the status of the message from each stage of accreditation – for example, (a) a statement, (b) a commonsense truth, (c) a principle, a standard, (d) a value, and (e) a transcendent symbol.

Reflecting this communication model, M. E. Spiro (1987, pp. 227–228) recognized four levels (corresponding to as many stages) in what he called the process of "internalization" of a concept or message:

1 Learn about a cultural reality or a concept (shared or rejected).
2 Accept it superficially, as a cliché (or stereotype).
3 Accept it as a belief.
4 Accept it as a salient belief.[47]

Various researchers (including D. Strang & S. A. Soule, 1998) have extended this effort, drawing attention to the role of promotion and institutionalization, and then ritualization of the messages.

Once again, this kind of exercise is theoretically seductive, but it presents a serious methodological problem: How does one establish reliable analytical criteria to express empirically each of these levels or each of these stages in order to avoid arbitrary conclusions?

Other such attempts run into no less substantial roadblocks. For example, P. Wheelwright (1955) proposed a three-stage process for the formation of a myth: the initial message goes through a "primary" stage, then a "romantic" stage, and, finally, a "maturity" ("consummatory") stage. This is a simple evolutionary pattern, with the first stage corresponding to premodern cultures and the last to "highly sophisticated cultures."

Whatever happens with those attempts, certain points of reference remain useful in the process of the emergence of myths. This is the case, for example, with the concept of institutionalization, which posits that at a given stage, the message has acquired a level of dissemination and recognition such that it is absorbed into the conventional mechanisms of acculturation and social control: the family, the neighbourhood, the school, the media, and the state. By which point the initial message, without having attained sacredness, is beginning to be taken for granted. The concept of ritualization evokes a similar state of advancement in the mythification process.

Another research strategy, also promising, consists in recognizing stages in terms of the progress of dissemination of the message among the population. This is the approach taken by P. Smith (2012, p. 748 ff.) in examining the influence of the idea of global warming: (a) the message becomes familiar outside the scientific community and fuels everyday conversations; (b) there is a dramatization of the message that becomes more pessimistic, suggesting apocalyptic scenarios; then (c) the message acquires the proportions of a general concern, and becomes a moral yardstick, especially among elites. To my knowledge, it is this kind of research that is best able to operationalize the steps inherent in the spread of a message.

But after all these efforts, the essential question remains: What mechanisms transform the initial message into a full-blown myth?

H. Social Actors

The final element in the mythification process consists in the work of familiar social actors such as governments, political parties, unions, the education system, churches, activists, social classes, and the media. For example, M. Frye (2012) has analysed the way in which, in Malawi, the combined efforts of the government, NGOs, and the schools instilled the cultural models that gave young people sources of motivation and aspirations that resembled the American Dream (dreams of professional success, work ethic, confidence in the future, etc.).

These actors, often leaders of social movements, instrumentalize the messages to establish their legitimacy, to better serve their interests, or to advance their agendas.[48] It follows that, to a large extent, the fate of social myths is a matter of power relations.

This statement applies not only to values and ideas but also to many other spheres of symbolic life. It has been shown, for example, that the introduction of baseball in the United States was closely associated with the growth of the business class; the sport reproduced its utopian world view at the same time that it gave its members legitimacy: one was supposed to find in baseball a safe place, close to nature, devoid of brutality, in which a community gathered in a verdant landscape, the action was subject to rules of equity, and heroes emerged from healthy competition (M. Nareau, 2007). In the same way, thanks to a long-standing, rich tradition of research, we know to what extent the content of great national narratives is defined and imposed by the conquerors, who usually erase the version of the defeated.

Social actors are therefore initiators and promoters of myths. The most powerful of them are able to win acceptance for the values, goals, and narratives that fit their goals, independently of their truth and their intrinsic morality. That is why it is important to identify the motives that drive social actors and govern the strategies of the mythification process.

This also explains why a social myth always presents two faces: officially, it promotes legitimate values and ideals, but this is hardly straightforward – it always also includes concealment and manipulation, serving less visible goals. For example, as we have seen, the myth of the American Dream glorifies responsibility, success, and the free expression of individual virtues, for the greater good of society. But at the same time, in the interests of the rich, it excuses glaring social inequalities and tends to shield the social order from protests.

Similarly, Mexican mestizos, in the name of equality, favoured the integration of Amerindians, but the hidden goal was to better establish their hegemony over the nation. Finally, most nationalisms instil solidarity, virtues, and love of homeland, but they also contribute to masking internal social divisions and power relations. From this perspective, a myth becomes an instrument, a strategic "resource."

According to the most predictable scenario, after its original expression, a message is taken on by a social actor that promotes it; other actors then join the movement to extend the influence of the message, hence the importance of its polysemy (see below). The relay function is also decisive in order to ensure accreditation, then institutionalization and ritualization of the message across a large segment of the population. The charisma shown by its propagators is another decisive factor. Finally, after mythification, the initial message has been incorporated into the mainstream culture so well that you can find traces of it in school, church, the media, advertising, songs, films, and so forth. At this stage, one can speak of ritualization.

Decisive here is the role of intellectuals (organic or otherwise, according to Gramsci's terminology). Regardless of their convictions, their goals, or their morality, whether they are considered simple adjuncts or autonomous activists, servants, or critics of the social order, what needs to be considered is that, when all is said and done, they are all acting as technicians or even mercenaries. They are expected to construct an effective argument, a mobilizing discourse.

As societal mechanisms, institutions ensure cultural and social reproduction. These organizations are both the conveyers and the guardians of beliefs, norms, codes, and customs. This is the role of families, schools, churches, governments, media, and courts. When, after intense operations of promotion and dissemination, the myth is finally taken on by institutions, the mythification process is very close to completion; its symbolic content is close to being taken for granted and becoming part of orthodoxy.[49] Conversely, formal institutions, as guardians of values and norms, need to ensure the support of the population in order to guarantee their functioning and their longevity. They do this by relying on powerful myths, objects of broad consensus.[50]

This being said, beyond initiatives by social actors and the mechanisms of acculturation, it is also necessary to recognize the significant work carried out more informally in popular culture and at the microsocial level (family, peer group, community). Although critical, this last dimension will not be dealt with much in this book, which is devoted mainly to the production of myth – what J. Kaufman (2004) calls the "post-hermeneutic" approach to culture.

Many studies conducted at the microsocial level have shed light on the complex interactions between the "producers" and the "users" of cultural content – M. Gottdiener's book (1985) is ground-breaking in this regard. The active role of individuals ("ordinary people") in value orientation and identity-building has been highlighted by different authors such as P. DiMaggio (1997), R. A. Peterson (2000), and T. Edensor (2002). This perspective emphasizes the role of redefinition and "negotiation," which are integral to the internalization of symbols. It is key to the research of Michèle Lamont, especially with respect to what she calls destigmatization strategies.[51]

Readers will recognize here the heritage of American anthropologist George Herbert Mead, who, distancing himself from the Weberian tradition, vigorously opposed the view that individuals passively absorb social values and norms. Studies have also shown that significant clashes can arise between the official meaning of a discourse and the meaning given to it by its proponents (for a striking example, see C. Gluck, 1985). The approach described above obviously remains open to these phenomena, which reveal the limited capacity of social myth to model consciousness and behaviours in the sense intended by the social actors.

By the same token, the approach proposed here does not in the least imply that cultures should be perceived as hegemonic, monolithic configurations requiring complete, uniform acceptance by all members of a society.

In light of the above, it should be understood that, strictly speaking, a myth is not solely a value, an ideal, or a belief. It is a collective representation that, as a vehicle of a value, an ideal, or a belief, has gone through all the stages of mythification to achieve sacredness. In this regard, I would point out once again the close connection between the analysis of this process and studies on social movements. To the extent that these movements need support from symbolic impulses, it is almost inevitable that they activate the mythification process. They are anchored in an "initiating" event (to use the expression of N. J. Smelser, 1962); they often tap into a negative, traumatic imprint; they play on emotion to build a consciousness and bolster a sense of belonging; they promote an ethos combined with an action program; they make extensive use of persuasion techniques; and they need credible leaders who embody the values and goals of the movement.[52] This being said, the fact remains that social myths are not inevitably associated with social movements.

Theories of cultural trauma contribute a rich perspective to the mythification process, as shown by many studies.[53] A study by R. Eyerman (2012b) showed how Harvey Milk, a municipal politician in the city of San Francisco assassinated by an antihomosexual activist in 1978, became a hero of the homosexual movement in the United States and was posthumously decorated (among other honours) with the Presidential Medal of Freedom by President Barack Obama in 2009. Interestingly, the analysis covers every component of the mythification process, from the initial injury to the "emotionally charged memory" and the "carrier groups."

In the same vein, E. A. Armstrong & S. M. Crage (2006) have shown how the 1969 Stonewall riots in New York came to embody the Gay Liberation Movement in the United States, while other similar events in Los Angeles, San Francisco, and elsewhere failed to reach the same national prominence. The authors find the explanation for this in various factors such as the role of "symbolic entrepreneurs" and persuasion, as well as commemorative strategies ("mnemonic capacity"). Once again, the analysis involves the main components of mythification. However, in both studies, the emotional thread that links the anchor to the ethos is treated rather superficially, as is the way in which traumatic events are used to construct and sustain myths.

I. Conclusion

A Four-Component Dynamic

Social myths are part of a collective dynamic comprised of four closely related components (see the diagram below).

These components are (a) collective imaginaries, of which arche-myths and myths are the main constituents; (b) the social actors, who control the sphere of production; (c) the target population(s) (the sphere of reception and appropriation, including adaptations and redefinitions); and (d) power relations and struggles, the outcomes of which weigh heavily on the fate of myth. This essay is nevertheless devoted mainly to components A and B, and the relationships between them.

Procedures and Spheres for the Application of the Model

Given the diversity of contexts, the forms that social myth can take on, and the combination of the conditions for its emergence, it is well-advised to consider the model of mythification as an ideal type. It follows, for example, that the order in which I presented the first five elements can change from one case to another. An emotion or an imprint can take shape before being crystallized on some element from the past – this is the case of a sentiment looking for an anchor. More generally, the model itself remains open to many variants.

That model also remains open to various levels or spheres of application. According to specific procedures, the mythification process can work at the level of the nation,[54] but also at the level of the family, the community, or even organizations. For example, it is clear that over the years, the image of the family takes on a sacredness sustained by emotional narratives transmitted by the oral tradition. One does not tarnish with impunity the memory of ancestors, close or distant, and we like to recall the aura that has emerged of their acts, even though their defects are well known.

Diagram 1. The mythical square

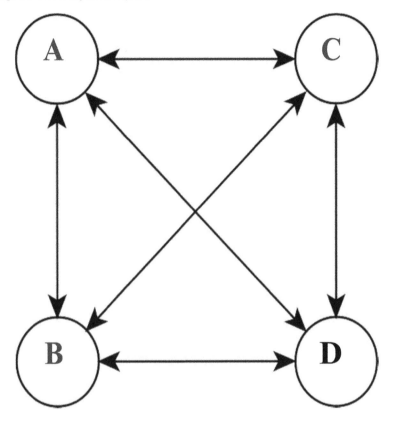

A Social myths as components of collective imaginaries grounded in archetypes
B Collective actors (production dimension)
C Target population (reception dimension)
D Power relations

With regard to organizations (businesses, associations, professional sports clubs, combat units in an army, etc.), sociological research has revealed the existence of a need for an identity – that is, for a sense of belonging and solidarity – created following the model of mythification: promotion of values transcending individual minds, celebration of episodes from a glorious past using commemorative rituals, which, in turn, generate an ethic of loyalty and a desire for emulation in a spirit of continuity, all of which is intended to inspire deep motivation and a drive to excel.[55]

Major league sports clubs illustrate this process perfectly. An eloquent example is provided in a recent book by P. Jackson (2013). A former coach of the Chicago Bulls and the Los Angeles Lakers (of the National Basketball Association), with which he won eleven championships, Jackson developed a coaching approach based on Buddhism. The goal of his philosophy was to raise team spirit not through religion but through spirituality – to foster a merging of individuals that induced each player to sacrifice himself for the sake of the team, for an "Us" bigger than the "I." A kind of transcendence was established in this way.

In a completely different domain, the canonization of literary works and works of art is strangely similar to the mythification process. Taking as an example *The Adventures of Huckleberry Finn* (1885) by Mark Twain, J. Arac (1997) explained how that novel came to be considered a great American classic largely because, at a critical moment in American history (1948–64), it promoted and embodied (especially among liberal whites) the fundamental values of the nation, conjuring up a sense of its founding destiny. It also embodied the nation's contradictions and ambiguities. Also instrumental in this project was the intense work of dissemination and celebration by various highly influential institutions (academies, schools, media, etc.). An equivalent in Quebec would be the activist work of Gaston Miron, who was recognized as the national poet by the time of his death in 1996; another is the heritage of the *Refus global* manifesto (1948).

Decline and Replacement of Myths

So far, I have described the essential components and aspects of the mythification process, whereby myth is presented as a sacralized ethos expressed in symbols. This model can serve as a useful analytical framework to account for the emergence and reproduction of myths, as well as their decline. The decline of myths is a subject that has attracted the attention of many authors. For example, P. Veyne (1983) formulated the following question with respect to the Greeks: How does one stop believing in legends, in Theseus, the founder of Athenian democracy, or in Romulus, the founder of Rome? Closer to home, the evolution of the Western world offers many examples of once powerful myths that have faded or have been completely erased. This is the case with men's superiority over women; with many of the great founding myths of Christianity (original sin, the punishment of Hell, etc.); with the hierarchy of races; and with the linear movement of history towards a purpose. Still other great founding myths are now showing their limitations, such as the idea of a universal morality, or of the free, rational individual, master of his destiny.

These examples allude to major changes at the international level, but national frameworks are teeming with similar episodes, albeit of more limited scope. Starting in the 1950s and 1960s, we saw both in Quebec and in English Canada a rejection of old national myths, in particular the one that defined the nation mainly in terms of its homogeneity and its organic relationship with the European mother countries. In Quebec especially, we saw the national identity dissociate itself from the rapidly declining Catholic religion. At the same time, Great Britain was relinquishing its myth of empire and the idea that it had a global mission. Germany, for obvious reasons, abandoned its myth of racial superiority and domination. Poland has experienced the ebb of a great founding myth, which saw it (like Romania) as the traditional guardian of Christianity against assaults from the Middle East. In the first decades of the twentieth century, under the impetus of Mustafa Kemal (Atatürk), Turkey largely converted to Western civilization, leaving behind its Muslim heritage. Many more examples could be mentioned that attest to the waning, disappearance, or rejection of social or national myths. We have also seen, almost everywhere, a decline in the idea of a chosen people vested with a providential mission.

Similarly, New Zealand currently offers the example of a powerful founding myth (the new Eden, the garden, environmental purity) that is now struggling against substantial increases in pollution, which have resulted in feelings of guilt.[56] One could also wonder, like O. Schell and J. Delury (2013), whether China will continue for long to find effective motivation in the myth of its past humiliations, given that it is now a major global power. Will it soon realize that these humiliations are now in profound contradiction with reality?

Clearly, a myth begins to lose its hold when one or more components of the mythification process no longer resonate closely with the social context. This can happen for various reasons: those components correspond poorly to the expectations, anxieties, and aspirations of the population; they are based on an insufficient persuasion apparatus; the anchor no longer creates the same emotion; the ethos has lost its sway; the alignment with praxis having broken down, the myth begins to have deleterious effects;[57] the social actors that promoted the myth are losing their power and credibility; significant elements of the context have changed (e.g., new contradictions, new challenges, new urgencies have appeared). Where social myths are rooted in praxis, any structural change at that level (in power relations, for example) will inevitably have symbolical repercussions.

It is likely that by the time any of these things happen, other myths are taking shape, competing with the old ones, and dislodging them because they better match the issues of the day or because they better serve the programs of the most powerful social actors. We have seen an example of this over the past few decades with globalization and ethnocultural diversification. New, powerful myths – such as openness to the world, pluralism and human rights, ecology and sustainable development, world peace and disarmament, equity between unequally developed nations, cosmopolitanism, neo-individualism – have weakened and even undermined the foundations of traditional myths in nations such as Japan (the exceptional nation that owes its collective virtues to its homogeneity and purity), and Israel (the small nation constantly under siege, but sustained by faithfulness to its eternal mission).[58] Similarly, in Quebec, the old myth of reconquest has perhaps weakened over the past few years (G. Bouchard, 2013a, part VI).[59]

The Criticism of Myths

Another question is related to the criticism of myths – more specifically, to the possibility of challenging them if they are viewed as harmful or contrary to the interests of a group. Given the power of social myths, one might expect the outcome of such an endeavour to be highly uncertain. One possible approach is to attack the symbols or identifiers of a myth. It has been alleged, for example, that by tearing down the Vendôme Column in 1870, the Communards in Paris shook the tyrannical, militarist bourgeois order (M. K. Matsuda, 2003). This is questionable. Undoubtedly, the destruction of symbols can help raise the masses' awareness and prompt critical reflection. But such an act leaves intact the symbolic, social, and political structure of the myth itself. That said, the erasure or destruction of symbols can expose the decline of the myths they embody.

In another direction, criticism of a myth can help call into question its empirical foundations (the anchors, for example) and thereby demonstrate the falseness or improbability of the narrative that supports it.

Such criticism can also bring out a myth's contradictions and expose its instrumentality – that is, its strategic dimension and hidden goals. Another approach consists in showing its deleterious or potentially dangerous effects.

But probably the most effective process, if one wishes to fight on a level playing field, is to combat the myth with another myth that is more mobilizing because it is more in accordance with praxis.[60] A shift thereby occurs that displaces the sacredness to other targets, other areas where the thirst for the absolute can be more effectively quenched, fears can be assuaged, and the archetypes can find other avenues, other forms of expression. However, a direct challenge to the ethos and the narrative can provoke strong defensive reactions, because it directly challenges the emotional substance of the myth.

Another approach is to avoid frontal attacks on the myth and instead try to modify it under cover of continuity, following the logic of recycling presented earlier in this chapter. This is what occurred in France in the nineteenth century. Having tried and failed to suppress regional languages and cultures in the name of republican homogeneity and unity, the leaders introduced the idea of small homelands ("les petites patries"), which would serve as microcosms of and preludes to the motherland ("la grande patrie"). According to the new republican discourse, the diversity of the regions now embodied and enriched the great symphony of France.[61]

Finally, from a more general perspective – one that could be associated with prevention – it has been shown that negative anchors based on traumatic events are especially powerful. Frequent sources of resentment, such anchors usually reflect violence by one population against another. However, this violence is always the extension of some form of radicalism. This is not an a priori condemnation of *all* radical positions; these can be justified and are sometimes even necessary (resistance to tyranny, for example). But one can see here an invitation to promote a culture of compromise rather than conflict, and an ethics of democratic consultation rather than of authoritarianism.

Creating Myths?

It is often asked whether it is possible to create myths. This chapter provides an affirmative answer. Every nation or society creates its own myths and then continually revises them. Even at the supranational level, recent history has given birth to powerful myths, as has just been mentioned. This statement, however, requires a significant qualification. First of all, a myth cannot be created out of thin air. The initial message has to activate an archetypal image through an operation that belongs more to translation or transposition than to construction or invention. Second, the myth has to be taken up by one or more sufficiently powerful social actors. Finally, given that myth must be connected to a praxis made up of anxieties, challenges, emergencies, and hopes, its promoters have to address conditions they only partly control, which imposes another limitation on the act of creation. This act therefore focuses on the parts in the mythification process that are amenable to the strategies and choices. In sum, the scope of invention is limited but remains substantial.

Western history over the past two centuries offers many examples of efforts to create new national myths or to restore old ones. Among the most spectacular of these was the growth of Italian fascism in the first decades of the twentieth century. This dramatic episode has been superbly analysed by E. Gentile (2005). Another example is offered by what is happening currently in Russia (Y. M. Brudny, 2013) and in most of the nation-states that emerged after the collapse of the Soviet Union. The cases of Ukraine and Belarus are especially instructive. These two countries have been striving over the past two decades to free themselves from the Soviet founding myths and to establish, among others, the myth of the golden age (lost because of Russian imperialism), and the great narrative of resistance to that oppression (A. Wilson, 1997).

Mythification: A Set of Choices

It would be a mistake to see in the stages or components of mythification any kind of determinism. All aspects of this process remain open and unpredictable. In terms of reception by the population, myth is not always a matter of a choice; but this is not true when it comes to its production. For those who are promoting a myth, the anchor is discretionary (there are no events that impose themselves), and so is the content of the ethos that sustains the narrative. These choices, moreover, are not made naively; rather, they are based on calculations and gambles, and nothing guarantees the success of the undertaking.

We find an example in Quebec with the attempt – mentioned earlier in this chapter – to make the Filles du Roy the female founders of the French Canadian nation in the eighteenth century. This feminist *and* nationalist interpretation has replaced a former moralistic version that made these immigrants models of virtue (after they had been depicted as prostitutes by some of their contemporaries). This effort is very recent; we can only speculate on its eventual fate.

Canadian politics recently offered another illustration with the Harper government's attempt to mythify the War of 1812 so that it would be viewed as a great victory, the memory of which would strengthen Canadian identity. For months, Canadians witnessed almost on a daily basis this promotion effort, whose aim was to raise a military conflict to the rank of anchor and imprint. The components of this campaign included a website, documentaries, historical re-enactments, a huge advertising offensive on several television networks (in particular during the 2012 London Olympics), the raising of a monument in Ottawa, and so on. In Quebec, the initiative was doomed to failure, given that Quebecers identify less with the Canadian imaginary. Also, the political intention was seen as too obvious and the process as too crude; the initiative was likened to a simple marketing campaign. It is uncertain how much effect it had in English Canada, but it generated quite a lot of criticism.

In fact, the chances of success of the Conservatives' 1812 project were always slim. First of all, it lacked substance, since Canada's role was rather secondary in that conflict, which was largely between Great Britain and the United States (J. Latimer, 2007; T. O. Bickham, 2012). Also, the Harper government was not the ideal promoter, given that its credibility was on the decline: by then, it was being criticized for its lack of transparency and for the liberties it had taken with the rules of democracy. It was also having difficulty finding powerful allies in civil society to support and extend its initiative.

But the main obstacle was to be found in a contradiction that tainted the project at its core. One of its main objectives had been to show that Canadians were capable of giving a black eye to the Americans on the battlefield. However, English Canadians pride themselves on being peaceable; for them, it is what distinguishes them from Americans, whom they tend to view (negatively) as violent and militaristic. So it is hardly surprising that the message had difficulty penetrating the imaginary, given the wrong imprint and the wrong ethos.

In summary, nothing guarantees that a message will reach the end of the journey of mythification, whatever the resources of the promoter. Some mythifications are more complete, and therefore more rooted and more effective than others, by virtue of a combination of favourable circumstances that are difficult to plan.

A Universal Sociological Reality: The Social Roots of Myth

So far I have dealt mainly with social myths in contemporary societies, but I have also considered premodern societies, especially to denounce the deep divisions that Western thought – partly under the influence of a prestigious anthropological tradition – created between the cultures of "primitive" societies and those of modern societies. This split gave considerable credit to the idea that myths are exclusive to the former, within which they take on features and operate under specific mechanisms from which the West has liberated itself through evolution. This orientation has impeded a careful study of the origins of myth as well as a better understanding of the mythification process. In this regard, the Western anthropological tradition has taken myth for granted in premodern societies, characterizing it as a structure of thought. It has also created a false discontinuity with contemporary societies.

I contend that the social roots of myth (especially divisions, conflicts, and power relations) are not fundamentally different in premodern and modern cultures and that the structuralist followers of Lévi-Strauss have diverted and impoverished research on premodern societies and cultures. The analysis of myths, wherever we encounter them, should be conducted through the prism of classical sociology, with particular attention to the social dimension. This would allow us to develop a better understanding of individual and collective behaviours, of social structure and change.[62] One would expect, somehow – with the inevitable adjustments required by contextual factors – the logic of mythification to be at work in all societies.

The clarifications above help distinguish among the three meanings that can be attached to the concept of myth. First, it can refer to the sociological mechanism. Second, it can refer to the symbolic content of which a myth is the vehicle. Third, the word also sometimes evokes the identifiers or symbols with which myth is associated (the "Kennedy myth," etc.). It is the first meaning that has been accepted for the purposes of this analysis.

Chapter Four

The Conditions for the Effectiveness of Myth

In any community, a message acquires a capacity for impact and influence according to the power of the actors who promote it and the effectiveness of the apparatus supporting mythification. Beyond the conditions already mentioned, this effectiveness depends specifically on a set of factors that I will present briefly.

1. A Coherent Definition of the Subject and the Territory

A clear definition of the Subject (the target population) circumscribed by a territory that enjoys a very broad consensus provides optimal conditions for mythification. This condition, in return, depends on how more or less fragmented the population is.

However, we know of cases – Acadia (Canada) or the Basque country, for example – in which the identity remains strong even though the Subject is difficult to identify precisely, especially in demographic and territorial terms.

2. The Archetypal and Cognitive Foundation

A myth is seen as likely to have a strong hold when it is closely linked to a powerful archetype and when it involves a wide range of discursive repertoires. Some archetypes are more capable than others of mobilizing minds. I am thinking particularly of the images of the traitor and the scapegoat, and of conspiracy theories in a context of insecurity and powerlessness.

3. Consistency

It is important that the message be formulated so as to seem free of contradictions, and that it project an image of clarity, simplicity, and strength, which is often achieved at the expense of nuance or accuracy. However, too much emphasis on coherence can be costly in terms of flexibility and thereby reduce the message's impact. As we will see, a dose of ambivalence and even of contradiction can prove beneficial here.

4. Empirical Basis

A myth is likely to be viewed as more relevant, and its narrative as more "true," when it is supported by data, even when those data, on closer examination, are fraught with inaccuracies.

5. Polysemy

The capacity of a message to include multiple resonances – and, accordingly, to convey meanings that are diverse, if not contradictory – facilitates consensus even when significant differences of opinion remain. For example, according to L. Kolakowski (2008), Marxism had enormous success thanks to the diversity of its message: it proposed an economic explanation for inequalities and conflicts, it offered an interpretation of the past and a vision of the future, it formulated new criteria for social ethics, and it suggested avenues for action (the struggle against the bourgeoisie, revolutionary protests). J. C. Alexander (2004) observed that, thanks to the powerful properties of polysemic configurations, different populations can come to share the same imprint resulting from traumatic events and suffering.

In the same vein, L. C. Olson (2004) showed how Benjamin Franklin himself contributed to his mythification by ensuring that the emblems that were supposed to represent him would carry different meanings from one public to another (in the American colonies, in France, in Great Britain, and in other countries of Europe). This process, as we know, remains a source of some confusion among his biographers. Similarly, progressive discourse in the United States has been used by liberals, but also by their conservative opponents (D. T. Rodgers, 1998).

During American presidential election campaigns, candidates (both Democrats and Republicans) often make the American Dream the foundation of their programs, as divergent as they are. To take examples from the recent past, both President Ronald Reagan and President Bill Clinton exploited this myth. Similarly, during the 2008 campaign, the "Stand up, America" of John McCain echoed the "Yes, we can" of Barack Obama. J. C. Alexander (2003, chapter 5) recalls that in American public debates, the same codes are used by the proponents of various perspectives on democracy. We observe a similar phenomenon in the abortion debate: the pro-life and the pro-choice sides resort to the same argument of individual rights and respect for human dignity.

Likewise, F. Polletta (2006) has demonstrated that narratives, stories, and anecdotes are better able to activate political and social movements when they convey a certain amount of ambiguity. It follows from this that a dose of polysemy is always useful and perhaps even necessary for a myth to succeed.[1] This is all the more important given that the initial message requires a double-appropriation – that of the social actors who endorse and propagate it, and that of the target audiences, which are always varied. Finally, note that the polysemy of a myth is also based on its capacity to become rooted in more than one anchor and to tap into more than one imprint. For example, the Shoah, originally associated only with the Jewish genocide, now carries resonance for all human beings. It has thus helped bring about a broad raising of consciousness on racial equality and the horror of genocides everywhere on the planet.

We should avoid confusing the polysemy of messages with that of the symbols or identifiers that represent them. It is well known that a single identifier can embody various messages successively or even simultaneously. C. Paces (2009) has shown how Jan Hus, in the former Czechoslovakia, originally symbolized the struggle for tolerance and freedom against the Catholic despotism of the Habsburgs. He was also used as a foil for the enemies of anti-Catholic heresy. Finally, in the eyes of Communist leaders, he embodied the birth of socialism and the defence of workers. Social actors and specific programs of action were associated with the promotion of each of these three visions.

In France, A. Jourdan (2004) conducted an analogous demonstration with regard to the memory of Joan of Arc, Napoleon, Bismarck, and others. Many similar studies have been carried out in the United States on Washington, Lincoln, and other major figures of the nation. We also know that the symbol of the Wandering Jew has been invested with many meanings across the centuries (L. Passerini, 2003). Some figures (such as William Wallace in Scotland) have embodied both triumph and defeat. In Mexico, the memory of Emiliano Zapata has taken on many meanings: bandit, messiah, soul of the revolution, homosexual, macho, mestizo, father of the nation, and so on (S. Brunk, 2008).

In Quebec, the figure of the poet Émile Nelligan has been invested with various meanings over the course of time: national poet, victim of the *Grande Noirceur*, the ideal of a noble culture that was able to resist Americanization, misunderstood genius, and so on (P. Brissette, 1998). This phenomenon has equivalents in all societies, with the most striking symbols being called upon for various causes, as if they had acquired a kind of autonomy from the message they were initially conveying.[2]

The polysemy of symbols cannot, however, be better illustrated than by the history of "Plymouth Rock," which recalls the founding of the United States by the Pilgrims arriving on the *Mayflower* in 1620. The rock on which the voyagers are said to have set foot when they landed was for a long time an inexhaustible symbolic source in the history of the country. But the associated meanings varied considerably: the stoicism of the Pilgrims, the escape from English tyranny, the vitality of Christianity in its struggle against intolerance, the promises of westward expansion, the defence of the freedom and rights of immigrants, and so on. Finally, it is interesting to note that today, the symbol is losing its hold, having been subverted by multicultural influences.[3] It has been supplanted by Ellis Island, the arrival point for many immigrants from the late nineteenth century to the 1950s.

6. Polyvalence

Closely linked to the previous one, this factor consists in a myth's power to serve very different – indeed, sometimes contradictory – causes and programs. Political and social life offers many illustrations. Polyvalence permits a myth to be adopted by competing social actors or by a plurality of actors who, independently of one another, find the myth advantageous, even if it sometimes means thoroughly reinterpreting the content of the message. The success of multiculturalism in English Canada can be explained this way:

- It satisfied the old elites, who felt the need to renew and bolster the cultural difference between Canada and the United States.
- It was a tool used by Prime Minister Pierre Trudeau and his allies, who wanted to weaken Quebec nationalism.

- It responded to the need for recognition felt by populations in the West, descendants of immigrants from Ukraine and Eastern Europe who had settled long ago on the prairies and who were uncomfortable with the bicultural definition of Canada as an anglophone and francophone country.
- It fulfilled the needs of industrialists, who were looking for immigrant workers.
- It pleased liberal minds concerned with pluralism and protection of rights.

One could conduct an analogous demonstration with respect to the important changes that occurred in the Quebec imaginary starting in the 1960s, and all episodes of profound changes in a society. Even a random and largely unpredictable combination of initiatives and interests can do much to shape the growth and destiny of a myth.

Regarding scientific paradigms or myths, a good example can be found in an anthology edited by P. Hall (1989) in which the authors show how the corpus of Keynesian ideas, as a broadly established paradigm, has been applied in various ways in a number of industrialized countries and has served very mixed socio-economic programs.

Polyvalence derived from the polysemy of myth, allows a de facto alignment of actors and interests that can strongly shape the minds of and changes in a society.

7. The Choice and Invention of Enemies

By identifying a specific population to unify and mobilize, myth creates a Them–Us boundary. When enemies are invented, or chosen from among already unpopular groups or populations, this facilitates the definition of the target population (the Subject) and creates conditions favourable to raising awareness of the message. For example, the myth of the chosen people or the universal mission always opposes, implicitly or not, a virtuous population to others that need to be converted. We also know that the founding myths of identity (family, regional, national, etc.) all include a large share of exclusion. The same is true of the great teleological myths, which are always based on a specific community or on a society faced with enemies. The archetype of the threatening Other is in full play here.

8. Adaptability

This refers to the capacity for a myth, through ceaseless redefinition and negotiation, to survive constantly changing contexts and challenges. This phenomenon has been illustrated by many studies – for example, on the evolution of the republican myth in France since the late eighteenth century (A.-M. Thiesse, 1997), and on the various reconfigurations of the frontier myth in the United States (R. White, P. N. Limerick, & J. R. Grossman, 1994).

9. Compatibility

A new myth does not automatically contradict already established myths and the common symbols, perceptions, and familiar narratives that are associated with them. Here I provide an example and a counter-example. For a good example of compatibility – at least analogically – we can refer to a study by V. Molnár (2005) on the introduction of modernist architecture in Hungary after the Second World War. The author demonstrates how it depended heavily on the structure of Hungarian society's symbolic field. As a counter-example, it has also been shown that the new national myths proposed to East Germans after the Second World War failed because they collided with the old popular myths supporting the collective memory (a past shared with the West) (M. Fulbrook, 1997).

   In other words, a dominant collective imaginary delimits a range of possibilities (and plausibility) and can impede the growth of new messages.

10. Relevance

This refers to a myth's capacity to connect with the anxieties and urgencies felt by a community at a given moment, so that the message becomes immediately meaningful to individuals by providing answers to nagging questions. The content of the message must match the needs and expectations of a population; that is, the message and the praxis need to line up. This condition includes a close link between the anchor and the imprint. It follows – as has been strongly argued by A. Swidler (1986) – that the context of a myth is as important as its content or its form. In this spirit, the growth of the Protestant Reformation can be closely associated with the political, cultural, and material context of the countries in which it triumphed: it brought solutions to the contradictions and problems they were experiencing (R. Wuthnow, 1989).[4]

Also relevant here is a message's capacity to overcome or circumvent the contradictions that an imaginary can contain in a given context. The myth of the "harmonious symphony" of France, mentioned earlier, is an illustration of this: it erased the apparent incompatibilities between the republican credo and the multitude of deep-rooted regional cultures. Finally, the match between a message and a context can be an effect of discursive strategies. Put simply, relevance hinges on the effective articulation of a tension, an articulation perpetuated through ongoing negotiations and adjustments among interacting elements.[5]

11. Piggybacking

This is an old and familiar process. A myth – especially an emergent myth – has the capacity to build on powerful myths and symbols already firmly established so that it shares their authority. This strategy of affiliation requires the myth doing the piggybacking to present itself as a natural extension, a corollary of other myths. The new myth can then expand by infiltrating other myths, using them as levers. The leaders of social movements often apply this strategy to bring about radical change. The objective is to soften the impact of the break by projecting these changes as part of a continuum, thereby making them easier to accept.

A spectacular example of piggybacking is provided by the Italian national liberation movement of the nineteenth century. The myths promoted to support this movement borrowed from very old myths built on family values (brotherhood, solidarity, honour) and Christian symbols (Christ as a saviour and a martyr, Mary as a virgin mother, etc.) (A. M. Banti, 2000, 2005). Yet these two symbolic threads had for a long time been at the heart of peninsular Italian culture. Again in Italy, the same threads were at work in the following century in the discourse of the fascist movement led by Mussolini. Likewise, in 1789 France, political leaders depicted the patriots as saints, as martyrs for liberty, and Jesus himself was presented as a revolutionary. Leaders spoke of Salvation, the Credo, and republican Commandments. There were also the Altar of the Homeland and the Trinity of the Republic; pilgrimages were established and liturgies were borrowed from Catholicism, but with Republican content (A. Soboul, 1983).[6]

Similarly, in Israel, the national renaissance in the twentieth century was based in large part on ancient mythical structures reinterpreted for contemporary mores (Y. Zerubavel, 1995). Russian socialism and communism borrowed from the orthodoxy of the Old Believers, whose social sensibilities and messianic faith thus found expression. Stalin justified his despotic power using the myth of the family: he was the father of the people. Italian fascism claimed continuity with the glories of the Roman Empire. In the journal founded by W. E. B. Du Bois (*The Crisis*), the lynching of blacks was likened to the crucifixion of Christ (A. H. Kirschke, 2007, chapter 3).

In Quebec, the discourse of the so-called Quiet Revolution in the 1960s sought to mitigate the impact of the break by showing that the new collective project (modernity, secularization, Americanity, etc.) aligned with the pillars of the francophone tradition, mainly language, religion, and nation.[7] In late-nineteenth-century Ontario, immigrant groups seeking integration and recognition tried to affiliate themselves symbolically with the founding Loyalists, who had come from the United States (R. Fair, 2006). I could cite many similar examples. More generally, references to sacred texts, eternal truths, and timeless principles (such as the laws of nature), as well as appeals to science, are means of establishing the legitimacy of a message.

Beyond myths per se, one can see here that piggybacking is a key technique of persuasion. This mechanism includes the possibility of not only connecting with another myth, but also becoming part of an overall mythical structure that supports an imaginary (see below).

12. The Nature of the Messenger

This has to do with the power, credibility, prestige, and resources of the messenger. The message is often taken up by a political party or social movement that is promoting changes to a discredited status quo. But this can also be done by highly respected institutional actors, who ensure the reproduction of firmly established myths or who endorse emerging myths. Alternatively, the true promoters of the myth can hide behind institutions that are supposedly virtuous and honourable, above any suspicion, such as the churches, philanthropic organizations, family associations, and prestigious universities.

13. Symbols (or Identifiers)

The process supporting the construction of a myth is usually hidden. It can be seen only through the symbols that embody it. Such a myth can centre on a triumphant figure offered as a model, or on a sacrificed hero whose tragic fate is the ultimate example of the values the myth is conveying. Who would dare to disparage Gandhi, Martin Luther King, or Nelson Mandela? This type of hero is particularly outstanding because of the energy and credibility associated with him.[8]

In the Quebec context, who would dare attack the image of the singer Céline Dion? She embodies the destiny of the traditional modest French Canadian, not too well educated, from a large family, raised in poverty, who thanks to her talent and courage nevertheless has achieved international fame without renouncing her roots, without betraying her people (she has remained simple, she talks casually to fans and reporters, she brags about her mother's *cretons* recipe, she is herself an exemplary mom, she is very much a "hometown girl"). Because of this loyalty, she has come to embody the two most powerful master myths of francophone Quebec: the fragile, disadvantaged minority, and self-affirmation in the spirit of reconquest.[9]

In much the same way, Maurice Richard epitomized through hockey the national struggle of French Canadians against English colonialism. The effect of this was amplified by the fact that Richard was a winner (with both his stick and his fists). Qualities were attributed to him that, at the time, were enough to absolve him of his violence on the ice: a good Catholic, from a very modest background, a devoted family man, a faithful husband, an exemplary parishioner.[10]

In another domain, still in Quebec, Premier René Lévesque in the 1960s became both the symbol and the inspiration for the struggle for the emancipation of francophone Quebecers, despite personal traits that would have been a disadvantage anywhere but in Quebec: short stature, raspy voice, unpolished manners, untidy appearance. Quebecers saw these characteristics as markers of his authenticity.

The symbol can also take the form of an event, an object, or a historical or archaeological site. Examples include Masada in Israel, Plymouth Rock in the United States (already mentioned), the Fossar de les Moreres in Catalonia, the Plains of Abraham in Quebec City, the Nazi concentration camps, the Plaza de Mayo in Buenos Aires, Dealey Plaza and the book depository in Dallas, and the photograph of the little Vietnamese girl burned with napalm. The tombs of unknown soldiers in various countries are also familiar figures. More recent examples are the symbolic exploitation of Tiananmen Square in China and the consecration of the site of the 11 September attacks in New York City (the famous Ground Zero). These two sites are being transformed into sanctuaries, each embodying in its own way the defence of freedom. A similar phenomenon is visible in the lives of certain individuals: think of the aura surrounding Nobel Prize laureates, Oscar winners, or those who witness the apparitions of saints.

In all of these examples, the symbol gives substance to the meaning conveyed by the myth. The myth extracts that meaning and grounds it in emotion. It thus gives it access to another existence and makes it more accessible to consciousness.

The fate of a symbol, like that of a myth, is based largely on its relationship to the context. Its characteristics must closely match the needs and expectations of a group or a population. We can see this in the United States with General Robert E. Lee, a prominent Confederate general whose image, for many decades, was celebrated on an equal footing with that of Lincoln in order to serve the urgent cause of national reconciliation after the Civil War. Ulysses S. Grant, who could have or should have been acclaimed as the conqueror, was paradoxically relegated to a secondary position (S.-M. Grant, 1997).

Finally, as noted earlier, the symbol gains strength from its capacity to convey many meanings at the same time, which allows it to expand its scope. Garibaldi, for example, carried simultaneously or successively the romantic image of the solitary hero; and the edifying, tragic image of the warrior sacrificed for the homeland; as well as the images of the generous knight, the great political strategist, the prophet, and so on (L. Riall, 2007).

14. Symbolic Merging

The choice of symbols or identifiers to embody the ethos is decisive. A symbol may acquire so much authority that it becomes completely merged with the myth or takes on a life of its own. Then it becomes the subject of celebrations, worship, and pilgrimages that amplify the message and can even result in a blurring or diversion of the original meaning. This is the case, as we have seen, with celebrated figures such as Washington, Napoleon, and Bolivar, and with objects such as the Nazi concentration camps, military cemeteries, and the *Mayflower*. We can thus speak of the myths of Caesar, Leonardo da Vinci, Lenin, and the Kennedys, when what is actually being referred to are the values or ideals (ethos) that gave birth to these symbols. The Shoah, a symbol of respect for human dignity and equality of races, is another example of merging.

In Quebec, even people who are not very familiar with hockey commonly talk about the myth of Maurice Richard. As we have seen, what these people are actually celebrating are the values and ideals he represents, in particular the virtues of the modest, courageous French Canadian who stands up to the English, thus embodying an aspiration at the heart of the national imaginary. Thus symbols can be characterized as magnified objects, overflowing with meaning and having more weight than material reality. This being said, there should be no illusion about this merger; myth is still key to the representation. The symbol always owes its authority to the work of mythification that it reflects.[11]

15. Reinforcement

This refers to a myth's capacity to draw support from auxiliary myths. For instance, L. Marx (1964) has shown how in the nineteenth century, American intellectuals (mostly poets and novelists) crafted pastoral myths designed to shore up major national myths such as the new Eden and the redemptive land, which were threatened by industrialization. In the same way, one could say that the myth of the American philanthropist bolsters the American Dream, which is a source of individual enrichment but also of deep social cleavages. The shortcomings of that myth are compensated for, if not obscured by, this other myth that invites us to see the future with optimism (the best is yet to come, the nation always knows how to reinvent and surpass itself, what is to come is more important than the past, the resources of the individual and the nation are unlimited, etc.).

On this basis, one could hypothesize that the myths of support or restoration are especially useful in the case of radical thought. This form of thought tends to suppress contradictory propositions, which can make it vulnerable.

16. The Power of Sanction

A myth will be subject to transgressions depending on the nature of the punishments incurred by offenders (from simple sarcasm to social exclusion and imprisonment, or even a death sentence). It is the institutional guardian of the myth that makes the difference: family authority, a community institution, a corporation, a church, a political party, a government apparatus. The power of sanction strengthens the immunity that sacredness gives to the myth. But the grip of the myth can at times be so strong that sanctions are imposed without any formal proceedings. For example, over the past two or three decades, how many politicians in the West have had to apologize and even resign after making remarks perceived as attacking gender equality, freedom of sexual orientation, racial equality, or other taboo principles?[12] In these instances, public opinion has played the role of guardian.

Anyone can easily test this mechanism with a group of friends, work colleagues, or students in a class. Just bringing up in an apparently neutral way a subject such as family violence against children, polygamy, eugenics, or incest can cause discomfort, even repulsion, and in all cases, there is a spontaneous reaction of rejection. What we often see is an inability to rationally justify this reaction (why exactly are polygamy and incest reprehensible?), since the established myth is so deeply anchored, emotionally embedded, and taken for granted.[13]

As we can see, the range of conditions that make a myth effective is very broad, and it is rare that a myth meets them completely. But when this is the case, a myth acquires a strength and maintains a hold that makes it an extraordinary cultural model – remember Albert Einstein's aphorism that it is more difficult to break a myth than to split the atom. This being said, let us ask another question, a highly empirical one: What are the signs that a myth is effective? I believe that various clues can be used; for example:

- First of all, its influence, which can be attested by its recurrent presence in public debates, in the life of institutions (political discourse, media, education system), in arts and literature, in various forms of commemoration, and in particular rituals; the myth then becomes overblown and enters the sphere of political correctness.[14]
- The longevity of the narrative, which can go through ups and downs but constantly resurfaces in various forms.
- The sense of belonging it arouses and the energy it creates, which come to light in individual and collective behaviours.
- The match between the message of the myth and (a) the orientations of political parties, (b) the policies of the government, (c) the ideologies of social movements, and (d) changes in society.
- The place of myth in identity, value systems, narratives, and world views.
- Its use as a lever in the service of other myths (piggybacking).

- The intense remembrance that occurs during a crisis or some traumatic event. A good example is the reaction of Americans after the 11 September attacks. Thanks to the mass media, a vigil was established from ocean to ocean, during which the citizens of that country ("like a family grieving," in the words of an NBC commentator) recited to one another their great founding myths, the values that sustained their unity, and the symbols that would permit them to overcome the ordeal they had suffered. Times of war are also fertile ground for this kind of manifestation. National holidays, in all countries, are also occasions for such remembrances.
- The response to the transmission of a myth as testimony to the existence of a taboo.
- The deep perceptions revealed by interviews with the population.

Conclusion

Cold Constructs and Warm Truths

As shown by the above, to the extent that they are strategically produced by social actors involved in power relations, social myths can be characterized as utilitarian constructs. However, once they have been internalized by individuals and made part of a collective imaginary, they take on a life of their own. This has led several authors to say that myths benefit from a kind of inertia or inner life, that they are not just products of social action. In fact, achieving this capacity is the crowning stage of mythification and confirms its hold.

From the sphere of production to that of reception (or appropriation), myths follow a course that transforms them from cold constructs into warm truths. We find an eloquent example in a study by E. A. Shils (1975, chapters 19 and 20) in which the author shows how military authorities are able to create strong primary feelings of solidarity among army units whose members, initially, had very little in common.

From that moment on, by virtue of the cognitive shift inherent in sacralization, these mythified representations are no longer merely effects of discourse or power. Rooted in the psyche, they have become powerful engines of identification, mobilization, action, and change driven by emotion, to the point that many individuals can subscribe to them without being aware of it. In this sense, W. L. Bennett (1980, p. 167) compared myths to the lenses in a pair of glasses: "they are not the things that people see when they look at the world, they are the things they see with." With regard to the social, myth, as a symbolic force, thus possesses a level of determination that amounts to a form of causality (see below).

On the Limits of Reason

If the fate of an idea, an ideal, or a message depends largely on its degree of mythification, then we need to question philosophical and political propositions that focus only on reason. This is the case, for example, with the constitutional patriotism promoted by the German philosopher Jürgen Habermas: a society governed by rational processes, the embrace of universal civic values as the foundation of collective life, containment of the irrational in private life. The chances of success – beyond a limited circle of intellectuals – of such a disembodied approach, with so little concern for the sociocultural determinants of the life of ideas, seem minimal. Indeed, what Habermas advocates overlooks a structural dimension of individual consciousness and a large part of what it owes to collective bodies. In one of his books (2001, p. 26), the German philosopher goes so far as to refer to the day when the mythical content of cultures is eradicated by the light of reason.

The model of constitutional patriotism is an attempt to examine the nation while attaching little importance to what constitutes its heart – namely, the whole identity dynamic and the non-rational from which so much of it is sustained. This includes the nation's powerful impulses of memory, belonging, and emotion, even where (as in France or the United States, for example) the nation is defined as "civic." At the risk of overstating it, one could say that this project seeks to think of the nation without the nation. In Europe, intellectuals who endorse Habermas's proposition have excellent reasons to be wary of the symbolic, affective content of the nation, given the recent history of that continent. But the nation basically remains what it is.

The non-rational aspect is precisely what, in the past, caused the failure of the loftiest schemes that appealed only to rationality. It is also what inspired and made possible the pursuit of noble ideals, along with the many achievements that today are part of human heritage. Obviously, in the interest of reason, there is an urgent need to better understand what the modernity of the Enlightenment tried to ignore and what always caught up with it somehow, most often tragically. This program was dangerous in that it allowed a great potential for backlash to generate in the shadows. Finally, such a program is misguided because it tends to push the non-rational down to a lower, harmful layer of consciousness. A more balanced view would also see in the non-rational a source of moral convictions, sensitivity, artistic and literary creation, altruistic impulses, loyalty to values, and access to various forms of transcendence.

There is also the fact that the track record of the nation is not all negative, far from it. At its birth and several times in its history, it was associated with the causes of democracy, equality, and freedom. Nothing shows this better than the history of Europe itself or the history of Third World decolonization. In these cases, nationalism was the driving force behind collective emancipation. Rather than the nation in itself and the myths that support it, perhaps we should be condemning above all the unscrupulous use made of myths by the ruling classes, those responsible for the nation's creation and destiny.

Precedence?

Social myths are a powerful mechanism for impelling or inhibiting the movement of a society. But this power does not entail any precedence over other factors or mechanisms. Myths operate through complex interactions in collective life. As noted earlier, part of myth is interwoven with power games related to contexts, whose outcomes are open to a range of possibilities. Another part is rooted in archetypical configurations that can be expressed in very diverse ways. Here we are in the domain of the flexible and the unpredictable.

In this spirit, we could ask whether myth, in itself, can ensure its survival in situations of adversity or if the role of social actors is crucial. I am inclined to endorse L. P. Spillman's (2003) answer to this question: it is in the combination of these two dimensions that the solution lies.

It does not follow that archetypes, however strong their impact on imaginaries, govern social thought. As matrices, they certainly delineate the range of invention and creativity; this can be seen with the restricted array of national myths or any discursive repertoire (G. Bouchard, 2013b). But they do not determine the content. In other words, as mentioned earlier, the archetypes provide a kind of keyboard on which the actors can compose.

Myth: Producer of Energy

These remarks are not meant to downplay the role of myth in the life of societies. There are, no doubt, depressive myths that act as inhibitors, that generate self-doubt and feelings of powerlessness, that lead to stagnation. I have given examples of these myths in the structure of thought of a few French Canadian intellectuals between the mid-nineteenth century and the mid-twentieth (G. Bouchard, 2003b, 2004b). But in the main, myths generate energy rather than lethargy. This power stems from the emotions they activate (the memory of a wound or an exploit), the psychological and moral security they provide (they alleviate anxiety, they feed aspiration), and the desire for transcendence they channel (in the quest for an absolute, for an accessible ideal). Myths also operate through identification with powerful symbols and through passion renewed by means of rituals. It can thus be understood that a society seeks to give itself founding myths; this reimmerses a society in the initial purity and energy of its origins, in the promises of birth – all of this, once again, independently of the more or less virtuous use that is made of myths.

The millenarian myth is one of the best illustrations of these mechanisms. It provides a coherent interpretation of the evolution of the nation; it outlines a direction for the future based on the memory of the golden age and the profound aspiration it conveys; and its realization is based on the responsibility and actions of individuals working in solidarity. Recall also Tocqueville's observation that the American myths, by stimulating feelings of equality and promises of success, encourage citizens to excel. This statement could be extended to all national myths, which are always used to unite and mobilize populations in the long term – the history of the Jewish population and its extension in the state of Israel are paradigmatic in this respect. Finally, we can refer to the many religious myths the function of which is to harness the energy of the gods, dreams, or celestial bodies – mainly the sun. Cannibal myths, which consist of ingesting the energy of the sacrifice victim, are similar in nature.

The Impact of Myth

Obviously, the primary impact of myth is in the immediate sphere of culture. As I have already pointed out, myths mitigate anxiety; they nourish identities, feelings of belonging, and loyalties by rooting them in emotion;[15] they perpetuate memory; they lay out avenues to the future; they feed ideologies and visions of the world; they structure religion; they uphold institutions; they mobilize populations; and they inspire scientific paradigms. They therefore act both on the structure of a society and on its course.[16] In *The Elementary Forms of the Religious Life* (1912), Durkheim maintained that a society ends up resembling the image it creates of itself. Similarly, we could say that in the long run, a society often ends up resembling its myths.

This statement reminds us of the significant changes in Quebec society starting in the 1960s. It is undeniable that these changes resulted in large part from a redefinition of identity brought about by a redefinition of national myths. Francophones began to perceive themselves as a majority in Quebec and not as just a cultural minority within Canada. This shift contributed greatly to building confidence and dispelling the self-doubt, fear of the future, and defensive reflexes that had been in evidence over the preceding century. At the same time, they redefined their memory to suffuse it with symbols of freedom, dynamism, and collective courage.

Besides mobilizing populations (for better or for worse), myths provide the symbolic foundation of the social – namely, a nucleus of values, references, norms, and codes thanks to which the members of a society can construct their identity, deliberate, arbitrate their conflicts, and build consensus. All of this enables them to overcome crises and traumatic events and resist external threats.[17] It certainly happens that these symbolic forces get derailed, but, as I have already pointed out, rationality by itself is hardly immune from abuses.

Myths influence the social in many other ways. They shape what B. Jobert & P. Muller (1987) call "referentials," which, like paradigms in science, inspire the economic and social policies of states.[18] It has even been shown that the conception and the management structure of railways in France and the United States were ultimately determined by the national myths of those two countries (J. L. Campbell, 1998). Many authors have maintained, moreover, that the political dynamic of societies is governed entirely by a symbolic structure under the hold of myth.[19] According to B. Baczko (1984), for example, each political regime must construct the (mythical) discourse establishing its legitimacy.

Finally, in various ways, myths interact with the economy, sometimes operating as a causal factor. For instance, the growth of francophone entrepreneurship in Quebec starting in the 1960s benefited from changes that occurred at the time in the system of values, political orientations, and identity. Powerful myths emerged, promoting modernization, social mobility, and national affirmation in all spheres of collective life.

The myth of the American Dream in the United States offers a similar example. First of all, that myth extolls the freedom of individuals and their capacities for initiative and development. It speaks of equality, with each individual supposedly starting with the same opportunities for advancement (in particular for getting rich). The same myth establishes that each individual is responsible for his or her own fate: what each of us becomes is a reflection not of an inequitable or biased social structure, but of the sum of the labour and talent we invest or manifest. Since individuals are thus completely responsible for their own failures and successes, they would be ill-advised to blame the social order. Meanwhile, those who grow wealthy are admired, for all of society benefits. Thus the myth favours enrichment and, indirectly, economic growth even while contributing to the acceptance of inequalities.

Three other examples illustrate the economic impact of myth, this time in a negative way with respect to growth or living standards. The national imaginary of Japan has for a long time been dominated by the idea that its great homogeneity (no more than 1 percent of the population is foreign-born) and its uniqueness were the source of its collective virtues; hence, Japan is not very welcoming to immigrants. Yet the very low fertility levels over the past several years are expected to result in a drastic decline in the total population (in the order of 30 percent) over the next thirty years. The Japanese elite is acutely aware of the enormous economic and social consequences unless serious efforts are made to revise national myths so as to open up the country to massive immigration (the possibility of a dramatic increase in fertility seems to have been ruled out). But in everyone's opinion, this would require a profound modification of the national imaginary, which would likely be met with strong resistance.

Research on 225 Amerindian communities in the United States (S. Cornell & J. P. Kalt, 2000) found that the economic or material situation of these populations is based far less on their natural resources or the labour market than on the quality of their governance and the vigour of their institutions. The study also found that these two factors depend directly on the strength of identity in those communities, on the state of their traditions and their continuity with the past.

The last example is the European Union, which is currently struggling with severe economic problems. Most experts agree that the solution to these problems is greater integration, which would provide the EU with monetary control mechanisms that are currently lacking.

According to this analysis, the EU has established a currency without equipping itself with all the instruments required to ensure its effective management. Greater centralization, though, is being hindered by the resistance of nation-states rooted in traditions and "local" feelings of belonging – that is, in the still powerful hold of national myths. Accordingly, many analysts are suggesting that the EU needs more powerful myths in order to counteract the strength of national myths and to bolster a sense of European identity, which is currently weak in many countries. This calls to mind the aphorism (apparently apocryphal) attributed to Jean Monnet, one of the fathers of the EU, who towards the end of his life is said to have declared that, if he could start over again, he would begin with culture.[20]

This discussion could be extended to include references as varied as Max Weber's theory about the economic influence of the Protestant religion, the studies that blame declining values for the collapse of the American economy in 2008–9, the symbolic conditions of economic development in many communities in Africa and Asia, analysis of the cultural foundations of the liberal market, and so forth.[21]

Chapter Five

Social Myths: A Pyramidal Structure

A. The Architecture of Myths within Imaginaries

Within any collective imaginary, it is important to distinguish two types of social myths: master myths and derivative myths.

Master Myths

Some myths take the form of fundamental symbolic arrangements that act as matrices, structure the culture of a society, and govern the formation of other myths. Sustained by the most enduring anchors and imprints, they express the society's strongest feelings: its fears, its hopes, its shames, its dreams. These are what I call master myths. This concept is close to the concept of core narratives or root paradigms that we find in the work of Victor Turner. It also recalls the axiomatic frames of B. C. Ray (1993, p. 95), as well as the mythomoteurs of J. A. Armstrong (1982) and A. D. Smith (1986, pp. 58–63). Finally, it is related to the concept of the "centre value system," which according to E. A. Shils (1975) contains the framework and ultimate beliefs that shape a society (as opposed to everything on the "periphery").[1] In each case, they are trying to designate a primary symbolic form with a structuring power that I see as similar to master myths.

With regard to Quebec, we can easily recognize here all the themes of the minority culture and its struggle to survive in America from one generation to the next – with the accompanying emotional and normative load. Perhaps this also brings to mind the sense of an unfulfilled national destiny (one that was interrupted in 1760), and of the desire – if not the duty – of reconquest associated with it, with all its corollaries of collective emancipation.[2] These two master myths are central to Quebec nationalism in its old versions as well as in the modern version that emerged from the Quiet Revolution.

In the same vein, we could mention Japan and its attachment to homogeneity and "purity" as the source of its collective virtues. In the case of China, there is the desire to overcome the humiliations suffered in the past at the hands of the West.[3] English Canadians feel a need to distinguish themselves from Americans by emphasizing their differences and moral superiority and so on. Every society can be the site of several master myths involving complex relationships.

Derivative Myths

Master myths change very slowly because they are built for the long term and because their structuring power ensures their resilience. They are also very closely linked to archetypes, the most deep-seated sites of the imaginary. However, they are periodically translated or retranslated into subsidiary myths that I refer to as derivative or secondary. These myths are better adapted to changing contexts and to the specific challenges or problems associated with them. In other words, these myths, constructed for the short or medium term, maintain the spirit of the master myths but remodel them according to eras or situations in order to perpetuate their hold and their effectiveness – in order that they can continue to produce meaning and energy.

We find in J. Campbell (1988, volume 1, parts 1 and 2; volume 2, part 1) a distinction between "primary" and "regressed myths," but this relates to a phenomenon different from the one I am describing here. Campbell was drawing attention to ancient myths that, over time, were transformed to give birth to new myths. He was also referring to firmly established myths in a given place that had been transformed by migrating to neighbouring territories. Working on the Caribbean, M. Laroche (1970, pp. 231–232 ff.) made this distinction by opposing what he called primary myths and secondary myths. The former, of European origin, were transplanted to the Americas, where they were reappropriated. Thus, here again, the distinction is based both on a geographical criterion (exogenous, endogenous), and a chronological or genealogical criterion (seniority).

To return to the example of Quebec, the two master myths mentioned above were subject to four or five translations from the second half of the eighteenth to the late twentieth century (G. Bouchard, 2013b). The most spectacular of these occurred in the 1960s with the Quiet Revolution, which gave birth to a highly effective set of derivative myths, including these: the collective recovery and assertion of French-speaking Quebecers in all spheres of social life (especially in business), anticolonialism, political autonomy (then sovereignty), the defence of the French language, the emergence of the "Québécois" ethnonym (sustained by Americanity, standing up to the symbols of submission and humiliation, freed from the paternalism of the French mother country), social equality, secularism, modernity, and democracy.

In the same vein, it has been shown that in the United States, the exceptionalist myth (I. Tyrrell, 2013), the myth of the frontier (R. Slotkin, 1986; R. White, P. N. Limerick, & J. R. Grossman, 1994), and the American Dream (J. Cullen, 2003) were also visible in various figures from the past, as is the myth of uniqueness and purity in Japanese history (S. Vlastos, 2013).

This process whereby derivative myths are generated from master myths is to a certain extent predictable, as illustrated by the case of Quebec. Since it was a small nation or community uncertain about its future, it is no surprise that it adopted master myths focusing on the values of unity and solidarity – values that were eventually expressed in derivative myths relating to the valorization of community ties, mutual aid, consensus building, collective mobilization, and aversion to anything that might cause division, fragmentation, and weakening. Whereas in a nation more sure of itself and that valorizes individualism, very different derivative myths are likely to form that centre on freedom, self-esteem, individual autonomy, competition, social advancement, and so on. Finally, where the quest for harmony and discipline is emphasized, one expects to see values such as social cohesion, tradition, the moral order, moderation, negotiation, and compromise celebrated.

A collective imaginary can thus be represented as a pyramid comprised of a relatively stable layer of master myths and a layer of secondary or derivative myths periodically redefined in accordance with contextual changes. This conceptualization makes it possible to clarify a familiar paradox by taking into account a double characteristic of myths, seen as both enduring and ephemeral. Derivative myths allow a society to adapt and change, sometimes at the cost of radical shifts, whereas master myths sustain the feeling of continuity that is essential to the equilibrium and survival of any community. These are the myths that, in the long term, ensure the perpetuation of the symbolic foundation of the social bond. Structured in this way, myths provide the symbolism a society requires in order to combine radical change and continuity.

The distinction between master myths and derivative myths also helps explain another paradox related to the hold of myths. We expect master myths to enjoy a strong consensus, whereas derivative myths are often subject to divisions and controversies (e.g., citizens can endorse different visions of democracy, justice, or equality).

Finally, derivative myths can themselves give rise to other myths, thereby playing in relationship to those myths a role equivalent to that of master myths. The pyramidal structure of myths within an imaginary thus takes the form of a sometimes complex stratification, as shown by the analysis of clusters (below).

Change

Change is introduced into this architecture at two main levels, each with its own pace and cost. We can anticipate that relatively frequent changes at the level of derivative myths are a source of tensions, conflicts, instability, and insecurity. So one can imagine the deep discomfort created by changes at the level of master myths. This can be seen currently in England, where the end of the Empire, entrance into the European Union, devolution, large waves of immigration, and urban riots – not to mention the foreseeable instability that the Brexit will bring about – have strongly shaken the nation's old symbolic foundations (less than one-third of adults living in the United Kingdom define themselves as British) and led to a broad-ranging search for identity.[4]

This can also be seen in Quebec, where various clues suggest that there has been a weakening of the myth of reconquest (viz. the collapse of the Bloc québécois, the decrease in support for sovereignty, the disarray – if not the crisis – within the Parti québécois following the 2014 electoral defeat, the appeal exerted by globalization on young people). Societies are usually reluctant to embark on such hazardous initiatives of redefinition, and they try to delay the process. For example, plenty of observers, both foreign and domestic, maintain that France is now facing a perilous leap because of the rigidity of republican myths (in their current version or interpretation) in the face of ethnocultural diversity.

We could also explain in this way why the great myth of racial democracy in Brazil has been able to survive its contradictions, in particular, its profound inequalities, most visibly in terms of race and region. The same applies perhaps to the myth of the American Dream to the extent that we currently see no mythical construct that can provide a substitute for it.

Clusters

Finally, certain master myths are, in fact, tightly integrated clusters of myths (comparable to mythemes),[5] something like constellations. This is perfectly illustrated, once again, by the American Dream, which is based on a complex assembly of auxiliary myths such as freedom (including responsibility), property rights, equality, individualism, the self-made man, competition, entrepreneurship, work ethic, and merit. The myth of the frontier, again in the United States, is another example of an aggregate, appealing to pioneer qualities, courage in the face of the unknown, manliness, virtues of the homestead and family solidarity, Jacksonian democracy, and the struggle of civilization against barbarism (Native peoples) and the wilderness.

The same is true for Quebec with the myth of (cultural) survival, born out of the failure of the rebellions of 1837–38. This myth summoned up various symbolic impulses: the fragile, threatened cultural and religious minority; the providential mission in America; the land as the crucible of French Canadian culture; and worship of the past as a reservoir of heroic deeds and heroes (often sacrificed) to be emulated. Other examples of clusters are the Israeli myth of the small besieged nation chosen by God and invested with a mission; the republican myth in France, focusing on the ideals of equality and universality under the paternal eye of the state; and, in Poland and Romania, the myth of the sacrificed guardian of Christianity, against the background of messianism.

These myths, like all master myths, are renewed from time to time in the form of derivative myths, which reproduce in their own ways the structure of the aggregate.

B. Archemyths, Antinomy, and Conflation

Finally, another structural characteristic of collective imaginaries relates to how prevailing myths are linked (or not) to one another. There are three possible situations. First, from time to time in a given society, it can happen that master myths (and their derivative myths), instead of appearing as juxtaposed, maintain complementary relationships and are combined around an idea or a crucial aspiration that functions as a matrix and catalyst; as a consequence, their hold and their effects are reinforced. Then any progress by one myth has positive repercussions on the others.

This vast symbolic configuration, which occurs only rarely in a society's history, but which profoundly affects its course because of the energy (and synergy) it produces, I refer to as archemyth. The emergence of an archemyth both reveals and favours rapprochement and even alliances among various social actors and their agendas. Indeed, the archemyth takes shape only if it can rely on a coalition of actors, while temporarily masking the major contradictions that affect any society. The archemyth thus has much greater range than the aggregate myth and operates at a larger scale, for it is based on an alliance of many myths, some of which may themselves be aggregates. However, myths that take the form of aggregates are integrated much more closely and in a much more enduring way than archemyths.

To take one example, a true archemyth has taken shape in English Canada in recent decades. Focusing on the double ideal of a decent society that is a moral exemplar for the world and of a society distinct from and morally superior to the United States, it is based on a coalition of master and derivative myths, such as non-violence, respect for diversity (multiculturalism), the quest for compromise rather than confrontation, social order (Charter of Rights and Freedoms), compassion (universal health care), equality (equalization payments), the pursuit of world peace (participation in UN international peacekeeping operations), and so on.

This archemyth was perhaps undone somewhat by the policies of the Harper government (militarization, restoration of monarchist symbols, cuts to social programs, refusal to strengthen gun control, the growth of religious conservatism, etc.). But we should not draw hasty conclusions; more time is needed to determine whether this was a temporary deviation or a strong tendency. In fact, the new Liberal government, elected in October 2015, lost no time in rescinding major Harper policies and restoring the Canadian archemyth.

Similarly, an archemyth took shape in Quebec at the time of the Quiet Revolution. The main myths associated with it gravitated towards the idea of the collective affirmation of francophones, in a spirit of recovery and reconquest. This idea was summarized mainly in the slogan "Masters in our own house," referring to the economic and social promotion of francophones and the rejection of the old forms of domination (what remained of political and economic colonialism, English-Canadian, British, and American capitalism, clerical power, etc.), and so on.

With respect to the United States, according to S. Seidman (2011), the equivalent of an archemyth emerged in the course of the country's history around the ideal of civic individualism. According to Seidman, it was through this symbolic matrix that gay rights, for example, were able to become normalized and incorporated into mainstream American culture.[6]

Finally, revolutionary upsurges are often driven by archemyths, as we can see with the cultural transformations that shook France during the three or four decades before 1789. The agitation that sometimes mobilizes a whole society and draws it into violent, destructive initiatives is obviously part of the same phenomenon.

In opposition to archemyths, the prevailing myths in a society may contradict one another, thus cancelling out their effects. This is characteristic of an antinomy situation. The history of Quebec, once again, offers an example of this type. The myth of reconquest works in the opposite direction to the myth of the fragile cultural minority in the Americas: the former inspires collective audacity and pushes forward, while the latter fosters caution, even fear, and sometimes inhibition. Interestingly, this idea can lead to a renewed vision of Quebec's past, one that is often reduced to conservatism and stagnation (until the 1960s). In reality, what we find is a complex history comprised of alternating periods of stability and change, stagnation and boldness, inwardness and exuberance. One can see in these contrasting movements a reflection of mythical antinomy.

Israel is another case in point. It is currently divided between its globalizing and secular aspirations and its old identity as the chosen people (P. Beinart, 2012). The same is true with Poland, which finds itself torn between tradition and modernity (G. Zubrzycki, 2013a). With late Meiji Japan, one finds another interesting case of antinomy with the difficulty of reconciling the cult of the Emperor with democracy, community spirit with individualism (C. Gluck, 1985). We can also think of traditional Russian society, which used to lie on two major axes of contradiction: the first opposing the Western and Slavophile currents, the second opposing within Orthodox Christianity the Old Believers and the reformers.[7] Likewise, there were two Spains, divided between a Catholic, conservative tradition and a liberal, anticlerical tradition (J. Alvarez-Junco, 2011).

What is important to highlight is the sometimes contradictory structure of mythical configurations and the effects this can have on a society's course.[8] This being said, recall that one of the many functions of myth is precisely to mitigate or circumvent contradictions.

Finally, strictly speaking, there is a third situation in which social myths are in a way simply juxtaposed or intersect randomly without giving rise to a significant, consequential configuration. I speak here of conflation. For example, in Quebec, the myth of sustainable development is a relatively recent addition to the collective imaginary, one that has no obvious relationship to the myths that have been established for a long time. The same can be said for pluralism and for a few other ideals conveyed by globalization that have not been forged in the course of the Quebec past. This phenomenon can be observed in the recent history of many countries.

General Conclusion

A Social Approach to Myth

A Challenge for Sociology

In this book, I have attempted to advance our understanding of social myths and the process of mythification. I have tried to tackle fundamental problems related to culture and society. It would be disappointing if sociology could not provide answers to these questions, but it would be even worse if it avoided dealing with them altogether. It is in this spirit that I have shared these reflections.

In a sense, and in a more immediate way, this book has sought to respond to crucial deficiencies observed by various authors. For example, according to K. A. Cerulo (2002, p. 2), "we still have to discover the factors that drive human groups to invoke specific concepts and frames, or to withhold certain formats and schemata at different historical moments or within divergent social situations." Similarly, S. Tully (2005) considers it urgent for us to analyse dominant myths, their functioning, and their effects.

Even more concretely, I am thinking of this appeal formulated by J.-P. Codol (1984): "We urgently need monographs which isolate the origins of a particular representation, its anchorage in a tradition and its development in popular lore, functional significance for the group which conveys it, and its relative importance in the social life of institutions and of people" (p. 241).

In this spirit, I wanted to define an approach that, within the world of culture, builds on the concept of the imaginary broadly construed, including the structuring forms that are archetypes, but that is also open to the particularities of contexts. Among the representations rooted in the imaginary, I focused my reflection on myths and on the social actors that construct and reproduce them using various discursive strategies. Finally, I have presented myths as the matrix within which religion, philosophy, ideology, utopia, novel, narrative, the social sciences, and even the so-called natural sciences find sustenance.

A Renewed Approach

While I do not claim to have met all the challenges I set myself, which would require a vast research program, I believe it would be useful to review the findings drawn from the analytical framework I have outlined:

- A critical examination of the primitive culture/modern culture dichotomy is needed. That dichotomy postulates the existence of two radically different regimes of myths that are impervious to comparison. I advocate instead a general approach to myth that highlights its social connections regardless of place, time, and discursive channels.
- The framework is aimed at promoting a definition of myth as a universal sociological mechanism that has been active in premodern, modern, and postmodern societies.
- It is pointless to ask whether we should promote or combat myths; whatever one thinks of them, they are a powerful sociological mechanism that, for better or for worse, contributes to structuring cultures, shaping consciousness, and charting the course of a society.[1] This requires a better knowledge of them so as to find ways to control their effects and curb their excesses.
- The proposed approach makes it possible to connect what one could call the downstream and the upstream parts of culture – namely, on the one side, the historical and social dimension of myth, and on the other, its deep roots, which are archetypes and other mental structures. The analysis therefore makes room for structures, actors, processes, and contexts.
- In doing so, it also brings out the specific contribution of the concept of the imaginary, especially in its relationship to the unconscious and myth.
- This approach throws light on the origin and production of symbolic forms and, more broadly, cultural patterns. It is not

enough to assert, as various authors have done, that cultural patterns are the product of shared experiences and resources, that they are socially constructed (by institutions, classes, interactions among actors), or that they are biologically incorporated in the brain's neurological structure.[2] In this regard, mythification opens up an avenue – among the many possible, no doubt – that permits us to go farther by examining the origins of certain cultural frames (or meta-frames).

- It makes it possible to identify, within the universe of collective symbols and representations, the specificity of social myths as sacralized representations. It thus draws attention to the hold that imaginaries have as largely unconscious configurations of images and symbols that sustain collective representations. It also brings out, beyond the influence of ideas, the power of the myths that sustain them.
- I contend that while reason is the main engine of thought, myth is the main engine of culture. Our approach therefore encourages recognition of the limitations of rationality, which is not the only means to promote a message, the others being emotions, images, and symbols.
- By attributing the emergence and reproduction of myths to the initiative of social actors involved in power relations, the approach makes ample room for the dimensions of conflict and change (origin, reproduction, decline, replacement), contingent on the dynamics of master myths and derivative myths.
- In addition to highlighting the pyramidal structure of collective imaginaries, the proposed approach suggests that the various components of social myths and their interactions should be considered.
- This book foregrounds the idea that, since they are combinations of socially created reality and fiction, and most often with a strategic aim, social myths should not be evaluated primarily according to their accuracy or their intrinsic truth, but in reference to their symbolic and social effectiveness as sociological mechanisms. Another reason to adopt this perspective is that the main purpose of social myths is to take a gamble on reality and not to be a reflection of it (e.g., to eliminate or reduce inequalities, to bring freedom). One does not ask whether the myths of world peace, democracy, and social justice are true or false; they are directions that are considered promising for thought and action, and they therefore belong partly

to reality and partly to a projection beyond reality. Assessment in terms of true or false is valid only if we consider myth solely as a narrative, a view that I reject. Finally, through these remarks, I am not denying the need to carry out a specifically normative assessment of myths, but only pointing out that this type of assessment belongs to another approach and that it can benefit from better knowledge of this mechanism.

• Starting from the concept of mythification, the approach proposes a broad field of investigation capable of clarifying the various aspects of the life of myths, in empirical and theoretical terms.[3]

• Finally, it draws attention to and encourages reflection on the process of sacralization, especially on what I call the cognitive shift.

Certainly there is still a lot to be done in order to validate and refine this approach. For example, the two faces of myth – the one that reveals and the one that conceals – need to be better understood. One can assume that they are in close interaction, but this relationship should be explored further. Similarly, there is still a lot to learn about the means for criticizing or destroying myths considered deleterious. Yet another enormous challenge is to investigate the new alliance between reason and myth. This idea may be surprising or even worrying for some proponents of rationality. However, to ignore the influence of myth would be to disregard its underlying and mostly unpredictable impulses. Addressing it might contribute to ensuring a better exercise of reason. This book is quite the opposite of an attack on rationality; it is aimed rather at better focusing its field of action and its authority. Finally, there is an urgent need to extend the theoretical argument of this book in various empirical investigations.

The Question of Causality

I have mentioned on a few occasions that myths possess a capacity for action and change, and even constraint, that amounts to a form of causality. A complex question is raised here, one that is part of the general problematic – never really resolved – of the relations between the cultural and the social. I hasten to add that the form of causality mentioned here is partial and that it eludes attempts at measurement and statistical demonstration. It is also partial in the sense that it always operates within interactions among various factors, some of which are cultural or symbolic (mythified collective representations), while others are strictly social (competition of actors in power relations), and yet others are more material, related to contexts (economic, demographic, geographic, etc.). The question of causality, in the literal sense, therefore implies a dual dimension with a cultural and a social side. In analytical terms, this duality is useful and even necessary, but if it is overly pronounced, it can become reductive and lapse into reification (see below).

This being said, it remains possible to construct the qualitative equivalent of a proof by relying on various elements of convergence, alignment, and cohesiveness, from which emerge configurations (gestalts) that establish not only a likelihood but also a strong plausibility. This can be attested, for example, by the observation of sequences of events or changes, by lasting associations between symbolic allegiances and actions (or behaviours), or by an accumulation of testimony by actors.[4]

It seems difficult to go farther in terms of "causality." Overall, the analysis must rely on reasonable approximations, significant concomitances, and a few legitimate postulates.

The Status of Culture in Collective Life

Beyond causality per se, it is useful to clarify the theoretical backgrounds that govern a very wide range of views (often irreconcilable) with respect to the place of culture and symbolism in collective life. Drawing from the classics of sociology (Marx, Durkheim, Weber, Parsons, etc.) and a review of recent literature in the United States, combined with various surveys of European literature, allows me to submit the following schematization.[5]

The vast majority of authors favour a dualist representation that takes various forms, such as, culture/society, culture/structure, culture/action. These are the three most frequent forms, but the dichotomy also manifests itself in the varied expressions that contrast, for example, archetypes and history, cognitive and social structures, ideologies and power, the aesthetic and the social, and so forth. There is also the duality intrinsic to the sphere of culture itself, which appears frequently in the social sciences. It usually contrasts a structural dimension with a peripheral one that is derived from it, namely, traditions, narratives, patterns of behaviour, and so on and so forth.

In each of these cases, a split vision of collective life is asserted, with culture always cast as an active component, remote from the social. For some authors, the cultural possesses complete autonomy and takes precedence over the social, which is seen as proceeding from the symbolic.[6] According to others, in keeping with the classical (or "ortho-dox") Marxist tradition[7] and other materialist currents emerging from sociology or economics, but also from anthropology (Malinowski, Mor-gan, Rappaport, and others), the opposite is true.

These determinisms are often toned down with authors who, for example, recognize a share of autonomy in the cultural but still view it as dependent on the social. The opposite position is just as frequent: without being determinant, the influence of the cultural is presented as considerable, sometimes even as a constraint (this would in par-ticular be the case with archetypes, cognitive structures, or myths). In this sense, culture, as a system of meanings, beliefs, and values indis-sociable from emotion, is seen as weighing heavily both on individual choices and on collective action, in particular through the mobilization inherent in social movements. In certain cases, as we have seen, it could exercise a strong influence on the economy. In turn, these latter two ori-entations make room for a multitude of variants, especially when they involve the actions of individuals, institutions, and classes.

Another category of authors favours a middle position, a search for balance characterized by flexibility. They typically resort to concepts such as interpenetration, interactions, reciprocity, homology, and cir-cularity. According to this view, for example, the economic is perme-ated with cultural content (values, perceptions, traditions, identity allegiances of the actors, etc.) and culture itself never operates in a kind of empyrean; it is always part of material or institutional combinations and contextual arrangements.

Finally, for other authors there are no dichotomies – the social is entirely included in the cultural. Therefore the question of causality is irrelevant, since collective life is no longer conceived of in terms of dual-ities: in any society, the structural foundations, the power relations, the material connections, and the driving forces of change are subsumed in the cultural. Among the dominant figures of contemporary sociology in the United States, Clifford Geertz and Marshall Sahlins are the most representative authors of this trend. We can also associate with them poststructuralist authors, the so-called deconstructivists,[8] and many proponents of the *cultural turn*. Some of the writings of J. C. Alexander can also be linked to this stance.

With regard to this schematization, my preference is for the middle path: neither culturalism, nor materialism, nor any a priori precedence for any factor or dimension at all. This choice is dictated first of all by the need to take into account the unpredictable aspects of collective life, due to its extreme complexity. In the same vein, one must recognize a certain capacity for freedom that must be attributed to individual and social actors. Second, there is no social activity that is devoid of meaning, just as there is no social fact that is not symbolically marked. But interpenetration does not mean merger; even less does it mean the establishment of any kind of magisterium. For example, one certainly recognizes in social actors a substantial influence, while acknowledging that their interventions must deal with cultural preconditions that are more or less favourable.[9]

Third, the suppression of all duality unduly limits the possibilities for the analysis of collective life. It eliminates causalities, interactions, and any truly dialectical approach. Researchers would also be deprived of the means to understand social change in all its components and manifestations. For analytical purposes, it is desirable to be able to dissociate culture from the other dimensions of the social (broadly construed), without either devaluing it or giving it any kind of primacy. In short, here as elsewhere, flexibility and a good dose of pragmatism are welcome.

To this in-between approach, which we could call dialectic (or interactional), I add an important element. Since its birth in the nineteenth century, sociology has constantly sought to devise a comprehensive approach to the social. This is what, in large part, has driven the search for an explanatory factor, one that it is believed can be found variously in culture, economics, geography, biology, or demography. But this search is usually oriented by rather subjective philosophical choices that are not completely lacking in arbitrariness. Without abandoning the pursuit of overall comprehension, sociology could set itself a more limited ambition – namely, the search for what I would call totalizing ways. This would involve recognizing that the social lends itself to many parallel comprehensive approaches, many angles, each outlining an encompassing itinerary, but none of which would exclude other, parallel itineraries. In addition, none of these trajectories would exhaust the range of possible itineraries.

In other words, contrary to the postulate that usually sustains the quest for a general theory, this approach builds on the idea that the social contains a plurality of intelligibilities, each one as legitimate as the others. They do not inevitably complement one another, nor do they really contradict one another; rather, they are superimposed on or added to one another. It does not follow from this that the social is fundamentally contradictory; simply put, the complexity of its structure and its movement is such that it impedes attempts at one overall, hegemonic comprehension. And it would be wrong to see this as an admission of failure; rather, it is a different way to enrich our understanding of collective life while echoing its true nature.

Social Myth: A Universal Sociological Mechanism

Social myths are a fascinating form of collective representation; at the same time, they are a fundamental sociological mechanism. But how this mechanism functions remains poorly understood. For the study of contemporary societies, one can no longer turn to the classical models from the anthropological tradition, which limited the study of myths to so-called primitive or archaic communities (also called uncivilized or undeveloped), and which bore the imprint of Eurocentric rationalist bias. As already noted, we must reject all of those evolutionary approaches that associate myth with ancient societies even while they grant modern societies the privilege of reason, the outcome of a long process of purification. This poses a twofold challenge: admit that there could be in the cultures of modern societies more myth than was believed, and, in the cultures of premodern societies, more rationality than we thought.[10]

The myths of today are not vestiges or relics of a bygone era, as asserted by Mircea Eliade as well as by Claude Lévi-Strauss (who saw in the modern novel the "debris of the mythological ice pack"); they are part of the mechanisms of any imaginary. Similarly, reason and emotion constitute a very old couple that belongs to the structures of the human mind. All cultures and all systems of thought (religions, cosmogonies, scientific theories, ideologies, etc.) are more or less effective alloys of myth and reason calibrated in various ways and focusing on specific goals. The mythical permeates both the culture of our time and that of the past, but it operates in different ways and in different forms.

Clearly, I am distancing myself from the approach developed by Claude Lévi-Strauss and his disciples, whose vision of myth focused primarily on the search for symbolic, rational symmetries (deep logical structures, formal reciprocities), thus neglecting the emotional component – which I consider fundamental – as well as any analysis of the social parameters of myth. The whole problematic of sacralization (and the cognitive shift) was, for them, absent, because they viewed mythical thought as a permanent, structural attribute of primitive societies.

I am also distancing myself from the structuralist tradition of C. Geertz (1973), which postulates that culture as a whole constitutes a coherent symbolic system, regulated by a supercode, unbeknownst to the social, as it were. I maintain rather that, for analytical purposes, the cultural can and should be distinguished from the social, but that these two dimensions should not be compartmentalized. I also assume that the cultural is the site of a complex assembly of coherences, disorders, and contradictions.

Myth: A Strategic "Resource"?

With respect to the constraining power of myth, manifested in particular in taboo, a thesis presented by A. Swidler (1986), among others, highlights the autonomy of individual action. This argument asserts that people make instrumentalized choices from a repertoire (or toolkit) of "symbolic resources" (language, traditions, norms, codes, narratives, beliefs, values, etc.) that every society makes available to its members. They are able to develop identity, ethical, or behavioural strategies according to the contexts in which they find themselves. One recognizes here a certain influence from rational choice theory.[11]

In this respect, I believe that myths, as symbolic configurations, stand slightly apart, since they have the power to influence minds to the point of sharply restricting the range of choices and sometimes even eliminating them – which does not mean, as I have noted, that they cannot be used strategically by collective actors involved in power relations.[12]

Regarding these individual strategic choices, they seem to be limited to the rather superficial dimensions of the ego. Moreover, the "symbolic resources" they appeal to also have a history. They too are produced socially, and to some extent they are part of the process of mythification.

There is no call here for a return to a Parsonian-like sociology that mechanically derived behaviours from a broad set of stable, ahistorical values. The goal instead is to highlight the weight of certain collective representations conveying sacralized, socially produced values that are in constant movement, in part under the influence of individuals or groups. It is also important to recognize different levels of influence and ascendancy exerted by values and beliefs. Some of these are more superficial and thus lend themselves more easily than others to strategic choices.

The approach to social myths presented in this book therefore in no way postulates that all dimensions of culture share the same capacity to impose themselves or to model consciousness by virtue of a supposed overall cohesiveness. My analysis is limited to myths as a specific mechanism and as one collective representation among others.

What emerges from all this is a complex geometry comprised of many closely related levels of analysis, one that places myths at the heart of a vast network of interactions. In fact, the approach I have presented involves four interacting levels:

1 Deep, archetypal images.
2 The myths (master or derivative).
3 Formalized culture (traditions, rituals, narratives, models, patterns, codes, etc.).
4 Social actors (including power relations, social movements, institutional mediations).

The Study of Myths: Social Relevance

Beyond the theoretical dimension, the analysis of social myths is a response to very concrete concerns. I have already listed various ways in which myths can influence the economy. I have also mentioned how they contribute to the symbolic capital that maintains any social bond. The functioning, dynamism, and development of a society depend in large part on this cultural foundation, which includes national myths. However, these are currently being called into question by globalization and by the sociocultural diversification associated with immigration. One then wonders: Are these myths being redefined, or are they declining? And if the latter, what will replace them?[13]

These questions are also closely linked to resistance. In Western nations and elsewhere, some sectors of the population are opposed to the ethnocultural diversity that results from immigration, which they view as threatening the values and identity of the host society. Global forces are making such change inevitable. How are we to strike a proper balance between the imperatives of diversity and pluralism? And what should we preserve within national traditions and myths? At stake here, in large measure, is the future of social integration.

National myths influence in many other ways the course of a society, as shown by the case of Quebec. New myths made powerful contributions to the changes in the 1960s and 1970s associated with the Quiet Revolution. I have already mentioned one of the most decisive symbolic reorientations – francophone Quebecers began to define themselves as a majority in Quebec rather than a minority in Canada. A similar task is currently required for Quebecers as a whole. Having realized their potential for change, most of the prominent myths of the Quiet Revolution have lost their hold on the collective imaginary. Accordingly, many citizens today have – rightly or wrongly – a feeling of a symbolic emptiness, a lack of references and mobilizing ideals.

Social myths could very well find another area of application around the theme of the nation. The literature on the origins of the nation and nationalism is currently divided between two major theoretical streams. According to one, called *primordialism* or *perennialism*, national sentiment is ancient; indeed, it is often difficult to trace its roots to a distant past. According to the other, the nation, as part of the symbolic framework of a society, is related to the development of capitalism in the eighteenth century. Its construction was thus dictated by the new economic system's need to expand. This is the *modernist* or *constructivist* argument. It seems to me that we could go beyond this opposition, using the perspective of social myths.

According to the first thesis, master myths are very old, it is no longer clear how they were constructed, and they have blended with what the authors call ethnicity. According to the second perspective, since mythification is more recent, its processes lend themselves more easily to analysis, which draws more attention to the instrumentality of myths, hence an observation bias. In short, a single mechanism seems to be operating on different timescales and, no doubt, according to specific processes. This view allows us to relativize a very pronounced theoretical polarization that could jeopardize the advancement of reflection on the nation.

The Strength of National Myths

The emergence of the nationalism in the West and its continued strength have led many authors (E. Gellner, A. D. Smith, B. Anderson, S. J. Mock, and others) to view it as a substitute for religion. They posit that religion has been in decline since the eighteenth century and has gradually become incapable of forming the symbolic foundation of societies. The nation has thus taken its place as the new matrix.

This reasoning seems flawed to me, because religion and nation belong to two different spheres. In fact, religion as a set of beliefs and symbols for a long time supported the life of collectivities. Historically, these collectivities have taken various forms: tribe, city, fiefdom, kingdom, empire, and so forth. The nation (or the nation-state) is the most recent of these forms. Observe here that in spite of a strong current of secularization, religion has remained very active in many contemporary nations, including those that are considered the most secular,[14] just as it has in all the other types of collectivities. So it is erroneous to assert that premoderns lived in a religious framework while moderns live in a national framework. To varying degrees and in diverse forms, religion is present in both kinds of societies. The religious was even one of the main foundations of the nation at its birth.

What should be coupled therefore is not the nation and religion, but the nation and the social myths that constitute its symbolic foundation. These myths are to the nation what religion was to other collectivities. Today's myths differ from the ancient ones (which they have largely replaced) in that they provide access to sacredness or transcendence without necessarily going through the religious. In summary, the nation is not sacred in itself; rather, it is sacralized through its myths – including its religious myths.

The claim that the nation has replaced religion relies on a deceptive metaphor that impedes our understanding of the relationship between these two realities. Using the same logic, we could view social class, and even family, as a substitute for religion, which in terms of theory is not very useful. Finally, it would be a mistake to invoke Durkheim to support this argument. He asserted a very close union of the religious and the social among premoderns; however, he did not go beyond his basic idea that religion legitimizes the social order even while producing it.

Myth: Capable of the Best and the Worst

I conclude with a comment that goes beyond the strictly scholarly dimension. This book has explored the exceptional power of social myths as well as the huge issues associated with them. We just have to think of the manipulations fomented by ultranationalisms and by the various forms of fundamentalism. Let us hope the sociological community grasps the urgency of better understanding how this strange mechanism functions, for it has the capacity to energize an entire society and – like the language of Aesop or like religion – to produce the best as well as the worst. By virtue of their roots in archetypes, social myths draw from the shadowy forces of the ego, which harbours the potential for violence and ugliness, but also for dignity and beauty. Two questions, then, must be added to the agenda of sociology: How can we prevent the abuses of this potential? And how can we promote its beneficial expressions?

Myths, even when they convey positive values (with respect to norms set forth in human rights charters or treaties), should always be subject to the utmost vigilance. This is in keeping with a proposition of L. Kolakowski (1989): we should be keen to both promote and criticize these myths to keep them from being perverted. There are hardly any other options, because the mythical lies at heart of the cultural and the social. There are no societies without myths; there are only societies that ignore them.

Notes

Introduction

1 I wish to thank Alain Roy, who over the past several years has been supporting and stimulating my reflections on myth, as well as the members of the group Successful Societies of the Canadian Institute for Advanced Research (CIFAR), in particular Peter Hall, Michèle Lamont, William Sewell, and Ann Swidler. I am also grateful to Nathan Glazer, Susan Hodgett, and Jean-Jacques Wunenburger for their useful suggestions. I have also benefited greatly from comments made following many presentations of my proposals when I have given papers and lectures in America, Europe, and elsewhere. This volume has been written as part of the programming of the Canada Research Chair in Collective Imaginaries, which I have held since 2002. I also received financial support from the Université du Québec à Chicoutimi and the Fondation de l'université du Québec à Chicoutimi.

2 We can find overviews and discussions in L. Spillman (2002), J. C. Alexander (2003), R. Friedland & J. Mohr (2004), M. D. Jacobs & N. Weiss-Hanrahan (2005), J. R. Hall, L. Grindstaff, & M.-C. Lo (2010), and J. C. Alexander, R. N. Jacobs, & P. Smith (2012), as well as in *Reviews in Cultural Theory*, www.reviewsinculture.com). Finally, M. Schudson (1989), D. Crane (1994), and W. H. Sewell (1999) remain very useful references.

3 See, for example, P. DiMaggio (1997).

4 See also J. R. Hall (1993).

5 I give this last concept a broader meaning by including all forms of social bonds that are established at the most varied levels: family, community, city, region, classes, nation, and so on. I also include the sociality that develops in institutions and organizations. As for the concept of society,

it should be understood in the sense of "global society," in reference to the sociological theory of Georges Gurvitch. In practice, this expression has traditionally been likened to the framework of the nation or the nation-state.

6 Brief overviews are presented in, for example, D. Crane (1994, chapter 3) and M. Lamont & M. L. Small (2008). According to J. C. Alexander & P. Smith (2001, pp. 2–3), sociology of culture presents culture as something that needs to be explained by external factors, taken from the social. Practitioners of cultural sociology view culture as autonomous, containing its own explanatory principle. I will come back to this.

7 This idea is found in many classical works in social sciences, but also in various more recent authors such as C. Castoriadis (1975) and D. Schnapper (1994).

8 For a brief overview, see G. Bouchard (2013c).

Chapter One

1 In a similar way, L. Gauvin (1996) already spoke of a "linguistic superconsciousness" to characterize the profound attachment of Quebec francophones to their language.

2 I qualify these representations as overinvested because they transcend other representations and because they draw their exceptional authority from an emotional and symbolic register that goes beyond rationality and is anchored deep in the psyche.

3 This sensitivity, as we know, is now widespread throughout the world. In Quebec, for example, the famous ecologist David Suzuki asked that the Gulf of St Lawrence be treated as a "sanctuary" (*Le Devoir*, 16 October 2012, p. 1).

4 This mechanism extends in various ways to different fields. For example, what respectable intellectual would publicly admit that he was profoundly bored reading masterpieces by Homer, Shakespeare, and Joyce? Or that he hated classical music and art museums? Or that the Mona Lisa looked silly to him?

5 See L. Kramer (2011, chapter 4).

6 For an overview, see, for example, J. Thomas (1998). It should be noted that the ideas put forward by these authors have not all enjoyed the same fate, for instance, Bachelard's project intended to construct a "physics" of images, with its laws and so on. (G. Bachelard, 1992).

7 There are nevertheless remarkable exceptions, for example, S. J. Mock (2012a).

8 Acronym of New York University and the London School of Economics.

9 To a large extent, the same diagnosis could be applied to historical science. For example, in a collection of policy essays on the future of cultural history (L. Hunt, 1989), we find only two brief references to the myths of Antiquity. Even in anthropology, in which it was dominant for such a long time, the study of myths has declined drastically since the 1980s.

10 This is one of the main arguments in the monumental book by H. Blumenberg (1985).

11 The title of this essay indicates a sociological reflection, but we will see that the historical dimension, inevitably, also plays an essential role.

12 In *The Anthropological Structures of the Imaginary* (1999), he also talked about the "rationalist and iconoclastic repression of this civilization." This theme is presented in detail in many of his books.

13 On the concepts of the sacred and transcendence, see chapter 3.

14 Jung was tempted to introduce a dynamic dimension into that concept. But the attempt inevitably failed. What gives the concept of archetype its specificity is precisely the fact that it designates unique structural forms since they exist in virtually all periods and all societies (H. Weisinger, 1964, p. 200–201). For a critical examination, see J.-L. Le Quellec (2013).

15 Note that Durand took an intense interest in archetypal forms to the extent of apparently giving them a kind of priority at the expense of the dynamic dimension (particularly in his early work). But he subsequently tried to formulate a more balanced vision that did justice both to deep structures and to historicity. Jung's archetypes also owe much to the work of German anthropologist Adolph Bastian, who in the nineteenth century introduced the concept of "elementary ideas," which, like archetypes, operated at the foundation of each culture.

16 This can refer to the immediate family, an ideal community, Eden, the mother's breast, and so on.

17 Much of the work on the imaginary studies how these deep symbolic forms structure literary and artistic expression. For a classic example among many others, see M. Bodkin (1958). The works of Northrop Frye are in the same vein. This remark is also valid for the collective representations inherent in daily life and in the spatial framework (the poetics of snow, night, or fire; the imaginary of fashion, foods, the street, cardinal points, the plain and the mountain, communication, and garbage; the mythical structures of TV series, advertising, etc.). Another example: the father–mother–son triangle, which is one of the great founding images of Western societies (C.-G. Dubois [2009, chapter I]).

18 On the concept of repertoire in American sociology, see M. Traugott (1995).

19 In ancient societies, it also inspired myths of creation and origins, the purpose of which was to reconnect with the emergence of life in its purity and its new energy (K. Armstrong, 2005, pp. 70–71). For an example from the Brazilian literature, see Z. Bernd (2007).

20 For example, A. D. Biemann (2009) was able to show how, in various forms, this theme structures modern Judaism, in the manner of a "grammar of beginnings."

21 Gilbert Durand called this historical and social aspect "mythanalysis." For him, this concept designated the contextual analyses that seek to identify the expressions of primary images (archetypes) in the historical and social movement (G. Durand, 1992) – or the particular expressions of universal forms, inscribed in institutions, traditions, and practices. Conversely, the mythocritic, by starting from literary or discursive expressions, retraces the archetypes that inform them. In short, we could say that mythocriticism and mythanalysis are distinguished in the same way as text and context.

22 Referring to this, geographers such as C. Raffestin and M. Bresso (1982) talk about "territoriality." Along the same lines, see M.-C. De Koninck (2007, p. 1).

23 See J.-J. Wunenburger (1995, pp. 97–103).

24 I use this concept in the very broad sense of a particular context or situation, namely, a shifting combination of power relations, interests, and constraints (material and other) that influences perceptions and shapes action. That definition, freely derived from the Marxist tradition, differs from many others, in particular that of C. Castoriadis (1975) who associates praxis with a vision of individuals as autonomous agents, capable of transforming reality.

25 For an illustration focusing on the history of Europe, see the impressive tableau painted by G. Durand (1996, p. 85–136). A similar portrait can be found in P. Sorokin (1970).

26 It happens that the two meanings can be found in the same author. Two examples among others: V. Grassi (2005, pp. 16, 18, 29, 34ff.), and P. Carmignani (1998). On this subject, see J.-J. Wunenburger (2006).

27 Here I agree with various scholars, including L. Boia (1998, pp. 49–50, 105–106), for whom even deep structures are steeped in history.

Chapter Two

 1 The same myth can also go successively from one state to another. In many of the new republics born between 1800 and 1830 in Latin

America, the myth of racial equality was a powerful motivation for collective emancipation, but was then used in subtle ways to camouflage discriminatory practices based on race (M. Lasso, 2007).

2 From archetypes to myths, we can recognize what Gilbert Durand calls the "anthropological path" (1980). These concepts are related to the "semantic basins" mentioned above, although their scope goes beyond the concept of social myth as I define it. But even in their most diverse forms, these symbolic constellations always draw from archetypes, which seem unlimited in their potential ("the well of mythical memory is bottomless" G. Durand (1996, p. 64).

3 To take one example, how many public figures in North America in recent years have had to make apologies or even resign from their positions after having made comments considered offensive regarding gender equality, sexual orientation, or racial equality?

4 For a discussion on the diverse ways in which power (political and other) can have an impact on culture and its productions, see J. R. Hall and M. J. Neitz (1993, chapters 7–8).

5 In the words of the poet Gaston Miron: "If anyone touches my tongue, I bite."

6 This is shown, for example, by the strong reactions to three essays published by Georges Dor with Éditions Lanctôt in the late 1990s. The author had, however, positioned himself on apparently solid ground: he attacked the mangling of the French language in Quebec by showing that it hindered the social advancement of members of the working class. On this topic, see L. Meney (2010, in particular Part III).

7 For example, we commonly see books on the "Canadian" literature published in English Canada in which there is barely any mention of Quebec francophone literature.

8 I am referring here mainly to *The Elementary Forms of the Religious Life* (1915).

9 These ideas are key elements of his great book *The Elementary Forms of the Religious Life* (1915). The general principle is summarized in É. Durkheim (1897–8).

10 P. Sellier (1984) proposed a six-point definition of what he calls ethno-religious myths, which, however, he associates mainly with premodern cultures.

11 On literary myths, see the argument of P. Sellier (1984). P. Brunel (1988, pp. 10–15) also proposed a definition, too broad in my opinion because it encompasses a very large part of the mythical world.

12 See also G. Bouchard (2007a).

13　In the physics of relativity, the shortest distance between two points is not a straight but a curved line.

14　This contradicts various texts by G. Bachelard (e.g., 1960) in which he declares that imagination and science have to be separated, that they are in competition. In other texts, however, he reaffirms the creative role of the image in the production of scientific thought (e.g., 1934).

15　It could also be shown that philosophy, that highly rational enterprise, cannot dispense with using myth to provide initial points of departure. See on this topic the comment by Luc Brisson in L.-A. Dorion (1999, 132–136 passim). The same can be said for all the social sciences.

16　The history of heliocentrism is very well known, thanks to the misadventures of Galileo. That of "raciology" is just as instructive. C.-R. Reynaud-Paligot (2006) showed how that theory, formulated in the nineteenth century by the Anthropology Society of Paris, was based on the postulate (very widespread in Europe at the time) of the hierarchy of races. Very early, many studies called this postulate into question, but without weakening its grip. Its institutionalization and its complicity in colonialist ideology provided it with supports.

17　B. Latour (1988) made the provocative suggestion that the evolution of contemporary physics is captive to a heavily subsidized international "priesthood" that is maintaining its foundations.

18　See, for example, the analysis by C. Rosental (2003) of the dissemination of Elkan's theorem on artificial intelligence.

19　For a more extended epistemological statement on the relationships between myth and science, see M. Gerhart & A. M. Russell (2002).

20　For example, C.-G. Dubois (2009, chapter 4) showed how ancient literature contributed extensively to spreading the concept of the Beyond.

21　I am thinking here of the great classics, pioneers of social criticism, such as L. Goldmann (1955), G. Lukacs (1989), M. Bakhtin (1987), and C. Duchet (1979).

22　In addition to McDonald's and Tudor's work, these remarks are based mainly on R. Girardet (1986), C. G. Flood (2001), R. Boer (2009), C. Bottici (2007), and J.-J. Wunenburger (2001). For an analysis predicated on the concept of imaginary, see also J.-F. Bayart (2005, Part II, pp. 122–232).

23　I am providing only one reference, but Campbell has developed his ideas in many of his books.

24　For a very eloquent example of myth as the driving force of ideology, see O. Schell & J. Delury (2013). They show how the myth of the humiliation long suffered by China at the hands of the West has shaped the ideological discourse of the government.

25 See, for example, J. Ellul (1973), J. Baechler (1976), J.-P. Sironneau (1995), and C. Bottici (2007, chapter 9).

26 See W. L. Bennett (1980).

27 We also find this trait in the excellent book by M.-D. Perrot, G. Rist, & F. Sabelli (1992).

28 For France in particular, P. Bénichou (1977) showed how romantic writers have celebrated the values of freedom, progress, and faith in science and the future. For Quebec, see, for example, J. Pelletier (1991).

29 For example, M. I. Steblin-Kamenskij and A. Liberman (1982), D. Bidney (1955), and G. Gusdorf (2012).

30 For a comprehensive discussion on the forms and functions of myth in premodern and contemporary societies, see M.-D. Perrot, G. Rist, & F. Sabelli (1992, pp. 40–45). See also M. Massenzio (2002, pp. 19–22).

31 According to his concept, rite refers intrinsically to supernatural forces (gods or demons) and operates through emotion. Myth comes at a subsequent stage to rationalize rite and provide it with a narrative (*An Essay on Man, The Myth of the State*).

32 See, for example, T.H. Gaster (1984) and R.A. Segal (1999, p. 37 ff.).

33 I have adopted these two concepts, commonly used in the literature, without ignoring their ambiguities. Concretely, how can we reliably distinguish between raised consciousness and mystification (or alienation)? With Marx, for example, how is it possible to demonstrate that inculcation of the revolutionary program with the working class belongs to the former while the world view disseminated by the bourgeoisie belongs to the latter? Obviously, the theory here is based on an ideological choice.

34 We would expect this element, like element 17, to appear more frequently. This low frequency is perhaps due to the unsystematic nature of my sample.

35 For a discussion of the polysemy of the concept of myth, see L. Honko (1984). For a very good overview of myth in various periods, from the perspective of various disciplines, readers can refer to J.-P. Vernant (1974, pp. 195–250), H. Blumenberg (1985), E. Csapo (2005), A. Von Hendy (2002), W. G. Doty (2000), R. A. Segal (1999), C. G. Flood (2001, chapter 5), and S. Leonard & M. McClure (2004).

36 For general surveys of myth and Greek thought, see M. Détienne (1981), B. Lincoln (2000, Part I), W. G. Doty (2004), C. Calame (2004), and L. Brisson (2005).

37 For example, those studied in France by R. Boudon (1986, 1990) and G. Bronner (2003, 2007).

38 Consequently, it is safe to bet that pleas, such as that of A. Maalouf (2000), to reject religious affiliation (in favour of a "human" identity) will have little effect.

39 These include W. F. Otto (1987), T. Mann (2005), C. Jamme (1995), M.
     Maffesoli (2005), J. Starobinski (2001), S. Toulmin (1990), and I. Buşe (2008).

Chapter Three

1 S. J. Mock (2012a, p. 97) also uses the concept of process of mythification,
    but restricts it to the establishment of what I call anchors (see below).
2 Various studies have been carried out on this subject. I will point out two
    in particular, one related to India (M. Debs, 2013), the other to Turkey
    (G. Türkmen-Dervisoglu, 2013).
3 On the millenarian cycle (or "triad") applied to national myths, see
    M. Levinger & P. Franklin Lytle (2001).
4 Mao's regime, which had "awakened" it, chose to restrict the work of
    commemoration to victims belonging to the working class (R. Eyerman,
    J. C. Alexander, & E. Butler Breese, 2011). On the "Rape of Nanking," see also
    J. C. Alexander & R. Gao (2012).
5 For other similar examples, see S. J. Mock (2012a, pp. 37–44).
6 See G. Bouchard (2012c).
7 See J. C. Alexander (2004).
8 This episode and the discourse around it were summarized by columnist
    Christian Rioux in three articles published in the newspaper *Le Devoir* (5, 6,
    and 7 August 2013).
9 In July 2014 there was a series of international conferences in Oxford (UK)
    with the theme "Apocalypse: Imagining the End."
10 It has been said that Koreans have been victims of hundreds of attacks
    from more powerful neighbours since the tenth century. With the shame
    and guilt also come a longing for new challenges, a quest for rehabilitation,
    and a culture of pride and honour (B. Schwartz & M. Kim, 2002).
11 Examples of traumatic events that generate feelings of suffering include
    the Serb defeat of 1389 at the hands of the Ottomans in Kosovo; the fall of
    Constantinople in 1453 (from the point of view of the Greeks); the Catalan
    defeat of 1714; and the American Civil War (D. G. Faust, 2008). Examples
    of glorious acts or positive experiences that are sources of valorization
    include the intellectual triumphs of classical Greece; the English victory at
    Trafalgar; the gaining of independence by colonized nations; the economic
    development of Japan; and, on a lesser scale, the success of the Seoul
    Olympic Games in 1988 and the victory of the South African team (the
    Springboks) in the Rugby World Cup of 1995.
12 Post–Second World War Japan is a prime example (A. Ashimoto, 2011).
13 V. Woolf (1925, p. 221) wrote that "it is common suffering, rather than
    common happiness, effort, or desire that produces the sense of brotherhood."

14 A recent book was, in fact, titled *This Republic of Suffering* (D. G. Faust, 2008).

15 Pascal (*Thoughts*) and Mikhail Bakhtin, in his famous book on Rabelais, wrote very beautiful passages on this subject.

16 This is what, it should be recalled, inspired Martin Heidegger to write his *Letter on Humanism* (1946).

17 See below in this chapter. See also G. Bouchard (2015, pp. 15–27.)

18 My concepts of imprint and ethos correspond quite closely to what R. Eyerman (2012a, p. 570) calls "emotional experiences" and "interpretative reaction."

19 Attempts to construct an ethos are always aimed at building consensus, something that, given the divisions present in any society, often requires complex contortions in discourse. In the United States, the creation of a monument in memory of the fallen of the Vietnam War provides a fascinating example. See R. Wagner-Pacifici & B. Schwartz (2002).

20 For a similar argument, see A. Pizzorno (1986).

21 This is similar to what R. N. Bellah (1970) calls – in a way that, however, introduces a certain confusion – "civil religion."

22 The secular conception of the sacred is close to that of the Greeks, for whom the perfection of the divine was not external to the universe, in which they recognized a symmetry that was the imprint of divinity (see also L. Ferry, 2002, 2006). On non-religious concepts of the sacred within the imaginary, see F. Laplantine (1974), R. Bastide (1975), J.-J. Wunenburger (2009, pp. 122–123), R. N. Bellah (1970).

23 My position on this point, which casts the narrative as an auxiliary of myth, is largely in accord with C. Bottici & B. Challand (2013, pp. 4–5 passim). Myths require narratives, but the narratives themselves are not myths.

24 I am thinking here of imprints inciting domination, hatred, fanaticism, dictatorship, or violence.

25 A. Luse & I. Lazar (2007) and their collaborators have found such healing collective practices at work in Eastern Europe since its liberation from Soviet dictatorship.

26 See, for example, J. Laplanche & J.-B. Pontalis (1988). However, the social sciences have also analysed the traumatic events as mechanisms that have the effect of relieving a group and even a society of a psychological burden. This is the approach taken by A. Luse & I. Lazar (2007).

27 Similarly, Émile Durkheim (1915) showed how, in so-called primitive societies, ritual was used mainly to maintain the vitality of religious beliefs and the symbolic structures of society.

28 For brief discussions on the consequences of the traumatic event and on the appropriateness and negative effects of commemoration, see also J. K. Olick (1999) and A.-M. Parent (2006).

29 For an analysis of the Vancouver Winter Games in 2010 along these lines, see S. J. Mock (2012b). On an analogous subject, but from a different perspective, see S. Kapralski (2012).

30 Again with respect to the history of Acadia, R. Rudin (2009) showed that the partnership of Pierre Dugua de Mons and Samuel de Champlain, co-founders Acadia in 1604, has also inspired different narratives (Quebec, Canadian, and American).

31 I am using it in the strict sense of "delimited ideational package" (F. Polletta & M. K. Ho, 2006, pp. 191–192). We can also refer to a more elaborate definition: "an interpretative schemata that simplifies and condenses the 'world out there' by selectively punctuating and encoding objects, situations, events, experiences, and sequences of action within one's present or past environment" (D. A. Snow & R. D. Benford, 1992, p. 137).

32 There is ample literature on the subject. Readers can read the ground-breaking book by E. Goffman (1974). Over the years, secondary concepts have been introduced, such as these: master frame, frame alignment, framing effect, frame resonance (D. A. Snow, E. B. Rochford, S. K. Worden, & R. D. Benford, 1986; D. A. Snow and R. D. Benford, 1988, 1992). It should be noted that, with Goffman, "framing" extends to the fabrication of the image that individuals want to project of themselves in a given context. For example, all of the people involved in social relationships are actors who create their own characters. In this case, "framing" is a synonym for performance.

33 For similar examples, see W. Gamson (1992) and G. Lakoff, H. Dean, & D. Hazen (2004).

34 But it is also said that it is instead the image of the house that plays the role of matrix (M. H. Raffard, 2013).

35 The meta-figure in the literary field plays a role analogous to that of the paradigm in the scientific field. On the above, see G. Bouchard (2004a). These attempts, however, aimed at identifying a structuring theme or symbol in a book or in the work of an author, are sometimes accused of reductionism.

36 Similar demonstrations can be found in J. Jenson & R. Levi (2013) and W. Kymlicka (2013). Those authors have shown how neoliberalism adopted (and perverted?) the discourse of human rights and multiculturalism (in the latter case, by making links between the citizen and the consumer).

37 The history of antisemitism best illustrates the effectiveness of this mechanism. We also know the role assigned to it by R. Girard (1983, 1986) in the founding and functioning of societies.

38 On this type of thought and the principle of the "included third party" as a dialectic way out of contradiction, see also S. Lupasco (1987) and G. Durand (1980).

39 Believing that our world was the worst possible, he suggested destroying within ourselves, by any means, the will to live.

40 See also P. Carmignani (2003).

41 This idea is an underlying facet of most of his books, in particular *Structural Anthropology, Tristes Tropiques* and *The Raw and the Cooked*.

42 See also M. Lamont (2002).

43 Various authors have mentioned the possibility of a grammar of the imaginary itself. But that is certainly a very distant prospect. In some of his books, Gilbert Durand (in particular 1999) posited the existence of a syntax and a semantics of images; he also toyed with the idea of a universal grammar of the imaginary. See also A. Pessin (2001, p. 215 ff.) and J.-J. Wunenburger (2006, p. 41 ff.). Somewhat along the same lines, there are also the seven regulation factors that, according to M. Angenot (1989), govern discursive exchange in a hegemonic context. From a more limited perspective, with respect to representations of the nation, O. Löfgren (1989) speaks of a grammar of nationhood. The same idea has a significant place in the works of Claude Lévi-Strauss.

44 The term piracy was especially appropriate in the colonies of the Caribbean, with their buccaneering past. The "miraculous weapons" evoked by the Martinique poet A. Césaire (1970) belong to the same vein. In Africa, the same metaphor is often used by the Algerian writer Kateb Yacine, among others.

45 See G. Bouchard (2000, chapter 7).

46 This kind of analysis owes a lot to the pioneering work by E. Laclau & C. Mouffe (e.g., 1985).

47 In an article from 1966 (p. 1163), the sequence included five stages.

48 This was shown by R. Eyerman & A. Jamison (1991). These actors are often called "carrier groups," in keeping with Max Weber's terminology. In American sociology, scholars also often speak of "symbolic entrepreneurs."

49 For a particularly successful illustration of the above, see P. G. Roeder (2007). Using examples taken from the recent past of nations (including the Soviet Union), the author demonstrates how the growth of nationalisms seems to be jeopardized without the crucial contribution of key institutions (which he calls the "segment-states") to activate and orient collective mobilization.

50 For example, referring to American society, A. Swidler (2002) showed that marriage, in order to last as an institution, must be supported by more

than just the desires of the two partners. There is ample literature on this subject, including material related to the Aboriginal populations of the United States (see, among others, S. Cornell & J. P. Kalt, 2000).

51 See, for example, a special issue of the *Du Bois Review* (vol. 9, March 2012). See also M. Lamont (2000) and P. L. Carter (2003).

52 On this, see D. A. Snow, S. A. Soule, & H. Kriesi (2004). Also, on culture and in particular identities as motivations of social movements, see D. McAdam, J. D. McCarthy, & M. N. Zald (1996).

53 Readers can refer, for example, to P. Sztompka (2000), J. C. Alexander et al. (2004), and R. Eyerman (2012b).

54 A fascinating example can be found in the book by M. Berezin (1997) on the growth of Italian fascism between the two world wars.

55 See, for example, J. W. Meyer & B. Rowan (1977), H. M. Trice & J. M. Beyer (1984), F. Dobbin (1994), and A. Haslam (2004).

56 For a more extensive analysis, see G. Bouchard (2013d).

57 J. Benda (1979, p. 33 ff.) applied this as a general theory of the life of ideas.

58 See S. Vlastos (2013) and Y. Zerubavel (2013).

59 There is an analogy here with similar phenomena at the individual level. Through work that it performs on itself in certain circumstances, the individual consciousness can orchestrate such substitution operations. This phenomenon has also been illustrated in fiction. Using a sample of North American novels, J. Thibeault (2015) has shown how the main characters redefined the roots of their identities (or the equivalent of their founding myths) independently of the traditional patterns prevalent in their community. The Ego is thus established as a new referent. Disaffiliation, (re)contextualization, and individualization are the key processes at work.

60 This was also suggested by K. Armstrong (2005, p. 133 ff.), referring in particular to the worst abuses of the twentieth century.

61 See J.-F. Chanet (1996) and A.-M. Thiesse (1997).

62 A. Cotterell (2004, p. 226 ff.) provides a few examples of profound symbolic changes brought about by conflicts or social disruption in tribal communities and in ancient times.

Chapter Four

1 A similar demonstration can be found in F. Polletta et al. (2011). Similarly, K. Thompson (2012) showed how ambiguities in Pentecostal discourse have contributed to its expansion by allowing practitioners to remodel the "official" meanings in such a way that they fit their needs and

idiosyncrasies. H. K. Bhabba (1994) also expresses appreciation for ambivalence and hybridity in discourse.

2 Many studies have shown that polysemy plays an identical role in the dissemination of ideologies, philosophies, or literary and artistic forms from one group or society to another.

3 This story was reconstructed in detail by J. Seelye (1998). Research seeking to identify the different and successive interpretations of a text also illustrates the polysemy of symbolic objects. For a remarkable example, see W. Griswold (1987).

4 See also D. A. Snow & R. D. Benford (1992).

5 This idea is also a key aspect of the book by R. Wuthnow (1989).

6 In many of his pioneering works, historian Albert Mathiez analysed in detail this dimension of revolutionary symbolism.

7 During the 1960 election campaign that brought the Liberals to power, this reformist party publicized its list of candidates by emphasizing the close links their families had with religion (brothers, sisters, parents who were members of the clergy, etc.). On the basis of a rather superficial interpretation of the gospels, the party also claimed that Christ, if he were to appear in the Quebec of the period, would have sided with the reformers.

8 For a noteworthy demonstration, see F. Utéza (2007). This study shows how, in the Brazil of the nineteenth and twentieth centuries, the idealized (even deified) figure of Lieutenant Tiradentes came to embody the republican identity of the country seeking its independence.

9 Other signs of loyalty: on her visits to Quebec, the star never fails to recall her attachment to her family (especially her mother), help little sick children, and refer to the familiar symbols of the old rural life of French Canada.

10 See, for example, B. Melançon (2006).

11 On the power of social symbols and its foundations, see, for example, M. Schudson (1989).

12 A recent example occurred in the United States in April 2014 when the owner of a professional basketball team (Donald Sterling) was forced to sell his football franchise and was banned forever from the league, besides receiving a heavy fine. He had been found guilty of practising discrimination and making racist remarks against blacks.

13 I have carried out the experiment a few times at public events. I asked people to remind me of the reasons why we have to be against incest. Few participants could come up with any credible arguments. But the reaction was always very negative, often aggressive. Just being asked the question disturbed people.

14 We have observed this phenomenon recently in Quebec with respect to the controversial Charter of Quebec Values bill proposed by the Parti québécois. The theme of gender equality has been used in every way imaginable by stakeholders – of which many are obviously new converts, which bears witness to the power of the myth.

15 See C. Bottici (2007, chapter 11).

16 We find a similar argument in G. Schöpflin (1997). All the work of British sociologist Anthony D. Smith on the nation and nationalism is also based on this idea.

17 This line of thought, which comes out of the Durkheimian tradition, enjoys a great deal of support in the contemporary social sciences. In addition to the already cited work of J. C. Alexander and his collaborators around the "strong program," I will mention just one key reference: A. P. Cohen (1985).

18 In the same vein, see J. Jenson (1989), P. Hall (1993), R. H. Cox (2004), M. R. Somers & F. Block (2005).

19 For example, W. L. Bennett (1980).

20 See, for example, V. Della Sala (2013).

21 On all these and other related subjects, see many relevant essays in D. Crane (1994), L. Spillman (2002), L. L. Tsai (2007), and J. C. Alexander, R. N. Jacobs, & P. Smith (2012).

Chapter Five

1 The literature of the social sciences contains many other related concepts, such as "emotionally rooted schemata" (Paul DiMaggio), " ideological substrates" (Georges Dumézil), "charter myths" (Bronislaw Malinowski), "sustaining myths" (Roy Andrew Miller), "master frames" (D. A. Snow), "deep images" (Alberto M. Banti), "overarching patterns" (J. R. Hall, Mary J. Neitz), "cognitive models" (John Meyer), "master tropes" (William Doty), "grounding myths" (R. Eyerman), "hypercodes" (Anna Triandafyllidou), and so on.

2 The Quebec national imaginary includes other master myths, but I will limit myself to these two for the purposes of this presentation.

3 At least with respect to the last century (Z. Wang, 2012). The Chinese refer sometimes to the period 1840–1949 (from the First Opium War to the founding of the People's Republic of China), and sometimes to a much longer period beginning with the Russian expansion into Siberia in the eighteenth century.

4 A search evidenced by, for example, the journal *Prospect*, which has long been edited by David Goodhart. See also C. G. A. Bryant (2006), K. Kumar

(2013), and I. Bradley (2007). According to research conducted by S. Fenton (2007), young people in England are rather indifferent to that uncertainty of identity. This feeling is no doubt characteristic of youth, since the discomfort aroused by the Scottish question, the difficulties of integrating immigrants, and membership in the European Union is persistent.

5 For many authors, this concept designates the constitutive units of a complex myth. For C. Lévi-Strauss, however, it refers to the basic principles common to all myths. I am using the former meaning.

6 The theme of civic individualism as archemyth is, however, only partly convincing since it does not integrate components as powerful as the American Dream, the melting pot, the chosen people, and exceptionalism.

7 The first axis of contradiction is very familiar; the second is summed up in G. Hosking (1997).

8 According to J. Hutchinson (2005, pp. 108–112), contradictions between national myths are beneficial for a society since they provide it with useful elements of flexibility, competition, and balance. But what is referred to by the concept of antinomy are more profound, irreconcilable divisions between master myths, which can inhibit the movement of a society, and not the symbolic richness inherent in the diversity of derivative myths and symbols associated with them.

General Conclusion

1 According to many authors – for example, N. Élias (1991, chapter 2) – myths should be completely eliminated. More realistically, we should instead see in this kind of appeal an invitation to develop the means to prevent the perversion of myths.

2 This idea is found among many proponents of cognitive sociology, for example, P. DiMaggio (1997) and B. Shore (1998). For a critical review of this scientific current, see B. Lahire & C. Rosental (2008).

3 This approach now guides my work in the field of culture. I have already drawn from it in a few recent publications (Bouchard, 2012a, 2012b, 2013a, 2013b).

4 In this sense, authors (e.g., J. C. Alexander, 2004, p. 12) talk about symbolic causality. See also J. C. Alexander (2013, p. 695), where the author also uses the concept of "causal sequence."

5 Readers will forgive me for not citing the too numerous studies on which the following schematization is based.

6 I recall Durkheim's famous aphorism: "A society ... above all is the idea which it forms of itself" (1915). One also thinks of C. Lévi-Strauss asserting the precedence of the symbolic over the social (for instance, in *The Savage Mind* [1966] and in *Mythologiques* [1969–81]).

7 I qualify this tradition as classical or orthodox because, since Gramsci, Althusser, Goldmann, Marcuse, and others, it finds itself in competition with other interpretations of Marxist theory that recognize a significant power for ideologies, narratives, myths, and other collective representations. We also know that Marx himself, in his later works, was more ambivalent about the respective weight to be accorded to infrastructure and superstructure.

8 I am thinking here of Jacques Derrida: "There is nothing outside of the text" (*Of grammatology*, 1976, p. 158).

9 This remark requires some qualification, for example, on certain aspects of the "power resource theory." According to this theory, the unequal distribution of power among social actors is responsible for the success or failure of political ideologies (see, among others, J. S. O'Connor & G. M. Olsen, 1998). In accordance with the approach outlined in this book, it is obvious that the collective imaginary, and especially dominant myths, inevitably come into play.

10 In a rare passage, C. Lévi-Strauss (1963, p. 230) himself pointed in this direction.

11 There is a great deal of literature on this subject. I refer to one title that is particularly representative of this analytical trend: M. Ganz (2000). The concepts of repertoire, toolkit, and individual strategic choices have been subject to many criticisms; see, for example, F. Cleaver (2002) and G. Sciortino (2012).

12 It can also occur that individuals act against their deepest convictions, but at the cost of feelings of transgression and betrayal that do not really have an equivalent in the collective sphere of power relations, where cold reason or *realpolitik* predominates.

13 A reflection on this subject can be found in G. Bouchard (2013d).

14 See A. Roshwald (2006, esp. chapter 4). See also R. N. Bellah (1970) and S. Mihelj (2007).

Bibliography

Alexander, J. C. (2003). *The meanings of social life: A cultural sociology*. New York: Oxford University Press.

Alexander, J. C. (2004). Toward a theory of cultural trauma. In J. C. Alexander, R. Eyerman, B. Giesen, N. J. Smelser, & P. Sztompka. *Cultural trauma and collective identity* (pp. 1–30). Berkeley, CA: University of California Press.

Alexander, J. C. (2013). Afterword. *Nations and Nationalism*, *19*(4), pp. 693–695.

Alexander, J. C. & Smith, P. (2001). The strong program in cultural theory: Elements of a structural hermeneutics. In Jonathan H. Turner (Ed.), *The handbook of sociological theory* (pp. 135–150). New York, NY: Springer.

Alexander, J. C., Eyerman, R., Giesen, B., Smelser, N. J., & Sztompka, P. (2004). *Cultural trauma and collective identity*. Berkeley, CA: University of California Press.

Alexander, J. C., & Gao, R. (2012). Remembrance of things past: Cultural trauma, the "Nanking Massacre," and Chinese identity. In J. C. Alexander, R. N. Jacobs, & P. Smith (Eds.), *The Oxford handbook of cultural sociology* (chapter 22, pp. 583–609). New York, NY: Oxford University Press.

Alexander, J. C., Jacobs, R. N., & Smith, P. (2012). *The Oxford handbook of cultural sociology*. New York, NY: Oxford University Press.

Alvarez-Junco, J. (2011). *Spanish identity in the age of nations*. Manchester, UK: Manchester University Press.

Anderson, B. (1983). *Imagined communities: Reflections on the origin and spread of nationalism*. London, UK: Verso.

Angenot, M. (1988). Pour une théorie du discours social: Problématique d'une recherche en cours. *Littérature*, 70, pp. 82–98.

Angenot, M. (1989). Le Discours social: problématique d'ensemble. *Cahiers de recherche sociologique*, 2(1), pp. 19–44.

Ansart, P. (1990). *Les Sociologies contemporaines*. Paris, France: Seuil.

Arac, J. (1997). *Huckleberry Finn as idol and target: The function of criticism in our time.* Madison, WI: University of Wisconsin Press.

Armstrong, E. A., & Crage, S. M. (2006). Movements and memory: The making of the Stonewall myth. *American Sociological Review*, 71, pp. 724–751.

Armstrong, J. A. (1982). *Nations before nationalism.* Chapel Hill, NC: University of North Carolina Press.

Armstrong, K. (2005). *A short history of myth.* New York, NY: Alfred A. Knopf.

Ashimoto, A. (2011). The cultural trauma of a fallen nation. In R. Eyerman, J. C. Alexander, & E. Butler Breese (Eds.), *Narrating trauma: On the impact of collective suffering* (pp. 27–51). Boulder, CO: Paradigm Publishers.

Bachelard, G. (1934). *Le Nouvel esprit scientifique.* Paris, France: Presses Universitaires de France.

Bachelard, G. (1960). *La Poétique de la rêverie.* Paris, France: Presses Universitaires de France.

Bachelard, G. (1992). *La Psychanalyse du feu.* Paris, France: Gallimard.

Baczko, B. (1984). *Les Imaginaires sociaux: Mémoires et espoirs collectifs.* Paris, France: Payot.

Baechler, J. (1976). *Qu'est-ce que l'idéologie?* Paris, France: Gallimard.

Bakhtin, M. (1987). *Epic and novel: Towards a methodology for the study of the novel.* Trans. C. Emerson & M. Holquist. Austin, TX: University of Texas Press.

Balandier, G. (1962). Les Mythes politiques de colonisation et de décolonisation en Afrique. *Cahiers internationaux de sociologie*, 33, pp. 5–20.

Banti, A. M. (2000). *La nazione del Risorgimento: Parentela, santità e onore alle origini dell'Italia unita.* Turin, Italy: Einaudi.

Banti, A. M. (2005). *L'onore della nazione: Identità sessuali e violenza nel nazionalismo europeo dal XVIII secolo alla Grande Guerra.* Turin, Italy: Einaudi.

Barthes, Roland. (1972). *Mythologies.* Trans. A. Lavers. New York, NY: Hill and Wang.

Bartmanski, D., & Eyerman, R. (2011). The worst was the silence: The unfinished drama of the Katyn massacre. In R. Eyerman, J. C. Alexander, & E. Butler Breese (Eds.), *Narrating trauma: On the impact of collective suffering* (pp. 237–266). Boulder, CO: Paradigm Publishers.

Bastide, R. (1975). *Le Sacré sauvage.* Paris, France: Payot.

Bayart, J.-F. (2005). *The illusion of cultural identity.* Chicago, IL: University of Chicago Press.

Beinart, P. (2012). *The crisis of Zionism.* New York, NY: Times Books/Henry Holt.

Bellah, R. N. (1970). Civil religion in America. In R. N. Bellah, *Beyond belief: Essays on religion in a post-traditional world* (chapter 9, pp. 168–190). New York, NY: Harper and Row.

Benda, J. (1979). *Discours à la nation européenne*. Paris, France: Gallimard.

Bénichou, P. (1977). *Le Temps des prophètes: Doctrines de l'âge romantique*. Paris, France: Gallimard.

Bennett, J. S. (2012). *When the sun danced: Myths, miracles, and modernity in early twentieth century Portugal*. Charlottesville, VA: University of Virginia Press.

Bennett, W. L. (1980). Myth, ritual, and political control. *Journal of Communication, 30*(4), pp. 166–179.

Bercovitch, S. (1978). *The American jeremiad*. Madison, WI: University of Wisconsin Press.

Berezin, M. (1997). *Making the fascist self: The political culture of interwar in Italy*. Ithaca, NY: Cornell University Press.

Berger, P. L., & Luckmann, T. (1967). *The social construction of reality: A treatise in the sociology of knowledge*. Garden City, NY: Anchor Books.

Bernd, Z. (2007). Le Nouveau-né. Mythe et contre-mythe dans les littératures des Amériques. In G. Bouchard & B. Andrès (Eds.), *Mythes et sociétés des Amériques* (pp. 23–47). Montreal, QC: Québec Amérique.

Berthelot, J.-M. (1988). L'imaginaire rationnel. *Cahiers de l'imaginaire, 1*, pp. 77–88.

Bhabba, H. K. (1994). *The location of culture*. London, UK, and New York, NY: Routledge.

Bickham, T. O. (2012). *The weight of vengeance: The United States, the British Empire, and the War of 1812*. Oxford, UK: Oxford University Press.

Bidney, D. (1955). Myth, symbolism, and truth. *Journal of American Folklore, 68*(270), pp. 379–392.

Biemann, A. D. (2009). *Inventing new beginnings: On the idea of renaissance in modern Judaism*. Stanford, CA: Stanford University Press.

Biron, M. (2000). *L'absence du maître: Saint-Denys Garneau, Ferron, Ducharme*. Montreal, QC: Presses de l'Université de Montréal.

Blumenberg, H. (1985). *Work on myth*. Cambridge, MA: MIT Press.

Bodkin, M. (1958). *Archetypal patterns in poetry: Psychological studies of imagination*. New York, NY: Vintage Books.

Boer, Roland (2009). *Political myth: On the use and abuse of biblical themes*. Durham, NC: Duke University Press.

Boia, L. (1998). *Pour une histoire de l'imaginaire*. Paris, France: Les Belles Lettres.

Bottici, C. (2007). *A philosophy of political myth*. Cambridge, UK: Cambridge University Press.

Bottici, C., & Challand, B. (2013). *Imagining Europe: Myth, memory, and identity*. Cambridge, UK: Cambridge University Press.

Bouchard, G. (1996). *Quelques arpents d'Amérique: Population, économie, famille au Saguenay, 1838–1971*. Montreal, QC: Boréal.

Bouchard, G. (1997). Quelques arpents d'Amérique: Les tenants et aboutissants d'une enquête. *Revue d'histoire de l'Amérique française, 50*(3), pp. 417–431.

Bouchard, G. (2000). *Genèse des nations et cultures du Nouveau Monde: Essai d'histoire comparée.* Montréal, QC: Boréal.

Bouchard, G. (2003a). *Raison et contradiction: Le mythe au secours de la pensée.* Quebéc, QC: Nota Bene/CÉFAN.

Bouchard, G. (2003b). *Les deux chanoines: Contradiction et ambivalence dans la pensée de Lionel Groulx.* Montréal, QC: Boréal.

Bouchard, G. (2004a). L'analyse pragmatique des figures et mythes des Amériques: Proposition d'une démarche. In G. Bouchard & B. Andrès (Eds.), *Figures et mythes des Amériques* [CD] (pp. 1–14). Montréal, QC: Université du Québec à Montréal.

Bouchard, G. (2004b). *La Pensée impuissante: Échec et mythes nationaux canadiens-français (1850–1960).* Montréal, QC: Boréal.

Bouchard, G. (2007a). Le Mythe: Essai de définition. In G. Bouchard & B. Andrès (Eds.), *Mythes et sociétés des Amériques* (pp. 409–426). Montréal, QC: Québec Amérique.

Bouchard, G. (2007b). Jeux et noeuds de mémoire: L'invention de la mémoire longue dans les nations du Nouveau Monde. In G. Bouchard & B. Andrès (Eds.), *Mythes et sociétés des Amériques* (pp. 315–348). Montréal, QC: Québec Amérique.

Bouchard, G. (2012a). L'imaginaire québécois, l'héritage de la révolution tranquille et le rapport Québec-France. In *La Coopération franco-québécoise: Hier, aujourd'hui, demain. Actes du colloque* (pp. 63–71). Toulouse, France: Privat.

Bouchard, G. (2012b). Collective destigmatization and emancipation through language in 1960s Québec: An unfinished business. *Du Bois Review, 9*(1), pp. 51–66.

Bouchard, G. (2012c). Un Épisode méconnu: La crise de la conscription et l'intervention de l'armée canadienne au Saguenay en 1917–1918. *Saguenayensia, 53*(2), pp. 5–18.

Bouchard, G. (2013a) Neo-liberalism in Québec: The response of a small nation under pressure. In P. Hall & M. Lamont (Eds.), *Resilience and neo-liberalism* (pp. 267–292). Cambridge, UK: Cambridge University Press.

Bouchard, G. (2013b). The small nation with a big dream: Québec national myths, 18th–20th centuries. In G. Bouchard (Ed.), *National myths: Constructed pasts, contested presents* (pp. 1–23). London, UK: Routledge.

Bouchard, G. (2013c). Pour une nouvelle sociologie des mythes sociaux. Un repérage préliminaire. *Revue européenne des sciences sociales, 51*(1), pp. 95–120.

Bouchard, G. (Ed.). (2013d). *National myths: Constructed pasts, contested presents.* London, UK: Routledge.

Bouchard, G. (2013e). Pour une histoire intégrante: La construction de la mémoire dans une société diversifiée. *Revue d'histoire de l'Amérique française, 66*(3–4), pp. 291–305.

Bouchard, G. (2015). *Interculturalism: A view from Quebec.* Trans. Howard Scott. Toronto, ON: University of Toronto Press.

Boudon, R. (1986). *L'idéologie ou l'origine des idées reçues.* Paris, France: Fayard.

Boudon, R. (1990). *L'art de se persuader des idées douteuses, fragiles ou fausses.* Paris, France: Fayard.

Bourdieu, P. (1986). *Distinction: A social critique of the judgement of taste.* Trans. Richard Nice. London, UK, and New York, NY: Routledge.

Bourdieu, P. (1991). *Language and symbolic power.* Trans. G. Raymond & M. Adamson. Cambridge, MA: Harvard University Press.

Bradley, I. (2007). *Believing in Britain: The spiritual identity of Britishness.* London, UK: I. B. Tauris.

Breuilly, J. (2009). Risorgimento nationalism in the light of general debates about nationalism. *Nations and Nationalism, 15*(3), pp. 439–445.

Brissette, P. (1998). *Nelligan dans tous ses états: Un mythe national.* Montréal, QC: Fides.

Brisson, L. (2005). *Introduction à la philosophie du mythe, tome 1: Sauver les mythes.* Paris, France: Vrin.

Brochu, A. (2002). *Rêver la lune: L'imaginaire de Michel Tremblay dans les chroniques du Plateau Mont-Royal.* Montréal, QC: HMH.

Bronner, G. (2003). *L'empire des croyances.* Paris, France: Presses Universitaires de France.

Bronner, G. (2007). *L'empire de l'erreur: Éléments de sociologie cognitive.* Paris, France: Presses Universitaires de France.

Brudny, Y. M. (2013). Myths and national identity choices in post-communist Russia. In G. Bouchard (Ed.), *National myths: Constructed pasts, contested presents* (pp. 133–156). London, UK: Routledge.

Brunel, Pierre. (1988). Préface. In Pierre Brunel, *Dictionnaire des mythes littéraires* (p. 7–15). Paris, France: Éditions du Rocher.

Brunk, S. (2008). *The posthumous career of Emilio Zapata: Myth, memory, and Mexico's twentieth century.* Austin, TX: University of Texas Press.

Bryant, C. G. A. (2006). *The nations of Britain.* Oxford, UK: Oxford University Press.

Buşe, I. (2008). *Du logos au muthos: Textes des conférences sur l'imaginaire et la rationalité.* Paris, France: L'Harmattan.

Calame, C. (2004). Du muthos des anciens Grecs au mythe des anthropologues. *Europe, 82*(904–905), pp. 9–37.

Campbell, J. (1970). Mythological themes in creative literature and art. In J. Campbell, *Myths, dreams, and religion* (pp. 138–175). New York, NY: Dutton.

Campbell, J. (1988). *Historical atlas of world mythology.* 5 volumes. New York: Harper and Row.

Campbell, J. L. (1998). Institutional analysis and the role of ideas in political economy. *Theory and Society, 27*, pp. 377–409.

Carmignani, P. (1998). L'invention du paysage américain. In J. Thomas et al. (Eds.), *Introduction aux méthodologies de l'imaginaire* (pp. 210–215). Paris, France: Ellipses.

Carmignani, P. (2003). De la contradiction et de ses modes de résolution dans la culture américaine. In P. Carmignani & J. Thomas (Eds.), *Hekateia: Au carrefour des savoirs,* volume 2 (pp. 203–220). Perpignan, France: Presses Universitaires de Perpignan.

Carter, P. L. (2003). "Black" cultural capital, status positioning, and schooling conflicts for low-income African American youth. *Social Problems, 50*(1), pp. 136–155.

Cassedy, E. (2012). *We are here: Memories of the Lithuanian holocaust.* Lincoln, NE: University of Nebraska Press.

Cassirer, E. (1946). *The myth of the state.* New Haven, CT: Yale University Press.

Castoriadis, C. (1975). *L'institution imaginaire de la société.* Paris: Seuil.

Cerulo, K. A. (2002). Establishing a sociology of culture and cognition. In K. A. Cerulo (Ed.), *Culture in mind: Toward a sociology of culture and cognition* (pp. 1–12). New York, NY: Routledge.

Césaire, A. (1950). *Discours sur le colonialisme.* Paris, France: Réclame.

Césaire, A. (1970). *Les armes miraculeuses.* Paris, France: Gallimard.

Chanet, J.-F. (1996). *L'École républicaine et les petites patries.* Paris, France: Aubier.

Chang, I. (1997). *The rape of Nanking: The forgotten holocaust of World War II.* New York, NY: Basic Books.

Chase, R. (1980). *The American novel and its tradition.* Baltimore, MD: Johns Hopkins University Press.

Cleaver, F. (2002). Reinventing institutions: Bricolage and the social embeddedness of natural resource management. *European Journal of Development Research, 14*(2), pp. 11–30.

Codol, J.-P. (1984). On the system of representations in an artificial social situation. In R. M. Farr & S. Moscovici (Eds.), *Social representations* (pp. 239–253). Cambridge, UK, and Paris, France: Cambridge University Press / Éditions de la maison des sciences de l'homme.

Cohen, A. P. (1985). *The symbolic construction of community*. London, UK: Ellis Horwood/Tavistock.

Corbin, H. (1958). *L'imagination créatrice dans le soufisme d'Ibn' Arabî*. Paris, France: Flammarion.

Cornell, S., & Kalt, J. P. (2000). Where is the glue? Institutional and cultural foundations of American Indian economic development. *Journal of Socio-Economics, 29*(5), pp. 443–470.

Cotterell, A. (2004). *Encyclopédie de la mythologie*. Bath, UK: Parragon Books.

Cox, R. H. (2004). The path dependence of an idea: Why Scandinavian welfare states remain distinct. *Social Policy and Administration, 38*(2), pp. 204–219.

Crane, D. (Ed.) (1994). *The sociology of culture*. Cambridge, MA: Blackwell.

Cruz, C. (2000). Identity and persuasion: How nations remember their pasts and make their futures. *World Politics, 52*(3), pp. 275–312.

Csapo, E. (2005). *Theories of mythology*. Oxford, UK: Wiley-Blackwell.

Cullen, J. (2003). *The American dream: A short history of an idea that shaped a nation*. New York, NY: Oxford University Press.

Debs, M. (2013). Using cultural trauma: Gandhi's assassination, partition, and secular nationalism in post-independence India. *Nations and Nationalism, 19*(4), pp. 635–653.

De Koninck, M.-C. (2007). Territoire et construction identitaire. In M.-C. De Koninck (Ed.), *Territoires: Le Québec: Habitat, ressources et imaginaire* (pp. 1–4). Quebéc, QC: Éditions MultiMondes.

Della Sala, V. (2013). Myth and the postnational polity. In G. Bouchard (Ed.), *National myths: Constructed pasts, contested presents* (pp. 157–172). London, UK: Routledge.

Demertzis, N. (2011). The drama of the Greek Civil War trauma. In R. Eyerman, J. C. Alexander, & E. Butler Breese (Eds.), *Narrating Trauma: On the Impact of Collective Suffering* (pp. 133–161). Boulder, CO: Paradigm Publishers.

Derrida, J. (1976) *Of grammatology*. Trans. G. C. Spivak. Baltimore, MD: Johns Hopkins University Press.

Détienne, M. (1981). *L'Invention de la mythologie*. Paris, France: Gallimard.

DiMaggio, P. (1997). Culture and cognition. *Annual Review of Sociology, 23*, pp. 263–287.

Dobbin, F. (1994). Cultural models of organizations: The social construction of rational organizing principles. In D. Crane (Ed.), *The sociology of culture: Emerging theoretical perspectives* (pp. 117–141). Oxford, UK: Blackwell.

Dorion, L.-A. (1999). *Entretiens avec Luc Brisson: Rendre raison au mythe*. Montréal, QC: Liber.

Doty, W. G. (2000). *Mythography: The study of myths and rituals*. Tuscaloosa, AL: University of Alabama Press.

Doty, W. G. (2004). *Myth: A handbook*. Westport, CT: Greenwood Press.

Dubois, C.-G. (2009). *Récits et mythes de fondation dans l'imaginaire culturel occidental*. Pessac, France: Presses Universitaires de Bordeaux.

Duchet, C. (Ed.). (1979). *Sociocritique*. Paris, France: Nathan.

Dumont, F. (1974). *Les Idéologies*. Paris, France: Presses Universitaires de France.

Durand, G. (1980). *L'Âme tigrée: Les pluriels de psyché*. Paris, France: Gonthier.

Durand, G. (1992). *Figures mythiques et visages de l'oeuvre*. Paris, France: Dunod.

Durand, G. (1996). *Introduction à la mythodologie: Mythes et sociétés*. Paris, France: Albin.

Durand, G. (1999). *The anthropological structures of the imaginary*. Trans. M. Sankey & J. Hatten. Brisbane, Australia: Boombana Publications.

Durkheim, É. (1897–8). De la définition des phénomènes religieux. *Année sociologique*, 2, pp. 1–28.

Durkheim, É. (1951). *Suicide: A study of sociology*. Trans. J. A. Spaulding & G. Simpson. London, UK, and New York, NY: Free Press.

Durkheim, É. (1915). *The elementary forms of the religious life*. Trans. J. W. Swain. London, UK: Allen and Unwin; New York, NY: Macmillan.

Edensor, T. (2002). *National identity, popular culture, and everyday life*. Oxford, UK, and New York, NY: Berg.

Eliade, M. (1960). *Myths, dreams and mysteries: The encounter between contemporary faiths and archaic realities*. Trans. P. Mairet. New York, NY: Harper & Row.

Élias, N. (1991). *Qu'est-ce que la sociologie?* Paris, France: Éditions de l'Aube.

Ellul, J. (1973). *Propaganda: The formation of men's attitudes*. New York, NY: Vintage.

Eyerman, R. (2001). *Cultural trauma: Slavery and the formation of African American identity*. New York, NY: Cambridge University Press.

Eyerman, R. (2012a). Cultural trauma: Emotion and narration. In J. C. Alexander, R. N. Jacobs, & P. Smith (Eds.), *The Oxford handbook of cultural sociology* (chapter 21, pp. 564–582). New York, NY: Oxford University Press.

Eyerman, R. (2012b). Harvey Milk and the trauma of assassination. *Cultural Sociology*, 6(4), pp. 399–421.

Eyerman, R., & Jamison, A. (1991). *Social movements: A cognitive approach*. Oxford, UK: Polity Press.

Eyerman, R., Alexander, J. C., & Butler Breese, E. (Eds.) (2011). *Narrating trauma: On the impact of collective suffering*. Boulder, CO: Paradigm Publishers.

Fair, R. (2006). Theirs was a deeper purpose: The Pennsylvania Germans of Ontario and the craft of homemaking myth. *Canadian Historical Review, 87*(4), pp. 653–684.

Faust, D. G. (2008). *This Republic of Suffering: Death and the American Civil War.* New York, NY: Alfred A. Knopf.

Fenton, S. (2007). Indifference toward national identity: What young adults think about being English and British. *Nations and Nationalism, 13*(2), pp. 321–339.

Ferry, L. (2002). *Qu'est-ce qu'une vie réussie?* Paris, France: Grasset.

Ferry, L. (2006). *Apprendre à vivre.* Paris, France: Plon.

Festinger, Léon (1965). *A theory of cognitive dissonance.* Stanford, CA: Stanford University Press.

Festinger, L., & Aronson, E. (1965). Éveil et réduction de la dissonance dans des contextes sociaux. In A. Lévy (Ed.), *Psychologie sociale II: Textes fondamentaux anglais et américains,* volume 1 (pp. 193–211). Paris, France: Dunod.

Fewster, D. (2006). *Visions of past glory: Nationalism and the construction of early Finnish history.* Helsinki, Finland: Finnish Literature Society.

Fisher, H. (2004). *La Planète hyper: De la pensée linéaire à la pensée en arabesque.* Montréal, QC: VLB.

Fisher, H. (2008). *Québec imaginaire et Canada réel: L'avenir en suspens.* Montréal, QC: VLB.

Flood, C. G. (2001). *Political myth.* London, UK: Routledge.

Friedland, R., & Mohr, J. (Eds.). (2004). *Matters of culture: Cultural sociology in practice.* Cambridge, UK: Cambridge University Press.

Frye, M. (2012). Bright futures in Malawi's new dawn: Educational aspirations as assertion of identity. *American Journal of Sociology, 117*(6), pp. 1565–1624.

Fulbrook, M. (1997). Myth-making and national identity: The case of the G.D.R. In G. Hosking & G. Schöpflin (Eds.), *Myths and nationhood* (pp. 72–87). New York, NY: Routledge.

Gamson, W. (1992). *Talking politics.* New York, NY: Cambridge University Press.

Gans, H. J. (2012). Against culture versus structure. *Identities: Global studies in culture and power, 19*(2), pp. 125–134.

Ganz, M. (2000). Resources and resourcefulness: Strategic capacity in the unionization of California agriculture, 1959–1966. *American Journal of Sociology, 105*(4), pp. 1003–1062.

Gaster, T. H. (1984). Myth and story. In A. Dundes (Ed.), *Sacred narrative: Readings in the theory of myth* (pp. 110–136). Berkeley, CA: University of California Press.

Gauvin, L. (1996). Glissements de langues et poétiques romanesques: Poulin, Ducharme, Chamoiseau. *Littérature, 101*, pp. 5–24.

Geertz, C. (1973). *The interpretation of cultures: Selected essays*. New York, NY: Basis Books.

Gentile, E. (2005). *The sacralization of politics in fascist Italy*. Cambridge, MA: Harvard University Press.

Gerhart, M., & Russell, A. M. (2002). Myth and public science. In K. Schilbrack (Ed.), *Thinking through myths: Philosophical perspectives* (pp. 191–206). London, UK, and New York, NY: Routledge.

Gienow-Hecht, J. C. E. (Ed.). (2010). *Emotions in American history: An international assessment*. New York, NY: Berghahn Books.

Girard, R. (1983). *Des choses cachées depuis la fondation du monde*. Paris, France: Le livre de poche.

Girard, R. (1986). *Le Bouc émissaire*. Paris, France: Le livre de poche.

Girardet, R. (1986). *Mythes et mythologies politiques*. Paris, France: Seuil.

Gluck, C. (1985). *Japan's modernmyths: Ideology in the late Meiji period*. Princeton, NJ: Princeton University Press.

Goffman, E. (1974). *Frame analysis: An essay on the organization of experience*. New York, NY: Harper Colophon.

Goldmann, L. (1955). *Le Dieu caché*. Paris, France: Gallimard.

Gottdiener, M. (1985). *The social production of urban space*. Austin, TX: University of Texas Press.

Granger, G.-G. (1996). *La Raison*. Paris, France: Presses Universitaires de France.

Grant, S.-M. (1997). Making history: Myth and the construction of the American nationhood. In G. Hosking & G. Schöpflin (Eds.), *Myths and nationhood* (pp. 88–106). New York, NY: Routledge.

Grassi, V. (2005). *Introduction à la sociologie de l'imaginaire: Une compréhension de la vie quotidienne*. Toulouse, France: Érès.

Griswold, W. (1987). The fabrication of meaning: Literary interpretation in the United States, Great Britain, and the West Indies. *American Journal of Sociology, 92*(5), pp. 1077–1117.

Gusdorf, G. (2012). *Mythe et métaphysique: Introduction à la philosophie*. Paris, France: CNRS.

Guttiérez, N. (1999). *Nationalist myths and ethnic identities: Indigenous intellectuals and the Mexican state*. Lincoln, NE: University of Nebraska Press.

Habermas, J. (2001). *The liberating power of symbols: Philosophical essays*. Cambridge, MA: MIT Press.

Hall, J. R. (1993). Sociology and culture. In J. R. Hall and M. J. Neitz (Eds.), *Culture: Sociological perspectives* (pp. 1–19). Englewood Cliffs, NJ: Prentice Hall.

Hall, J. R., & Neitz, M. J. (1993). *Culture: Sociological perspectives*. Englewood Cliffs, NJ: Prentice Hall.

Hall, J. R., Grindstaff, L., & Lo, M.-C. (Eds.). (2010). *Handbook of cultural sociology*. New York, NY: Routledge.

Hall, P. (Ed.). (1989). *The political power of economic ideas: Keynesianism across nations*. Princeton, NJ: Princeton University Press.

Hall, P. (1993). Policy paradigms, social learning, and the state: The case of economic policymaking in Britain. *Contemporary Politics, 25*(3), pp. 275–296.

Haslam, A. (2004). *Psychology in organizations: The social identity approach*. London, UK: Sage.

Hayward, K. (2009). *Irish nationalism and European integration: The official redefinition of the island of Ireland*. Manchester, UK: Manchester University Press.

Hentsch, T. (2002). *Raconter et mourir: Aux sources narratives de l'imaginaire occidental*. Montréal, QC: Presses de l'Université de Montréal.

Hermoni, G., & Lebel, U. (2013). Penetrating the "Black Box" of "Remembrance Day" playlist: Bereavement and the induction mechanisms of globalization—a study in cultural sociology. *Nations and Nationalism, 19*(1), pp. 128–145.

Hirschman, A. O. (1991). *The rhetoric of reaction: Perversity, futility, jeopardy*. Cambridge, MA: Belknap Press of Harvard University Press.

Hirsh, F. (2005). *Empire of nations: Ethnographic knowledge and the making of the Soviet Union*. Ithaca, NY: Cornell University Press.

Holguin, S. (2002). *Creating Spaniards: Culture and national identity in Republican Spain*. Madison, WI: University of Wisconsin Press.

Honko, L. (1984). The problem of defining myth. In A. Dundes (Ed.), *Sacred narrative: Reading in the theory of myth* (pp. 41–52). Berkeley, CA: University of California Press.

Hosking, G. (1997). The Russian national myth repudiated. In G. Hosking & G. Schöpflin (Eds.), *Myths and nationhood* (pp. 198–210). New York, NY: Routledge.

Hunt, L. (Ed.). (1989). *The new cultural history*. Berkeley, CA: University of California Press.

Hutchinson, J. (2005). *Nations as zones of conflicts*. London, UK: Sage.

Jackson, P. (2013). *Eleven rings: The soul of success*. New York, NY: Penguin.

Jacobs, M. D., & Weiss-Hanrahan, N. (Eds.). (2005). *The Blackwell companion to the sociology of culture*. Malden, MA: Blackwell.

Jamme, C. (1995). *Introduction à la philosophie du mythe, tome 2: Époque moderne et contemporaine*. Paris, France: Vrin.

Jenson, J. (1989). Paradigms and political discourse: Protective legislation in France and the United States Bbefore 1914. *Canadian Journal of Political Science / Revue canadienne de science politique, 22*(2), pp. 235–258.

Jenson, J., & Levi, R. (2013). Narratives and regimes of social and human rights. In P. A. Hall & M. Lamont (Eds.), *Social resilience in the neo-liberal era* (pp. 69–98). Cambridge, UK: Cambridge University Press.

Jo, S.-S. (2007). *European myths: Resolving the crisis in the European Community / European Union*. Lanham, MD: University Press of America.

Jobert, B., & Muller, P. (1987). *L'État en action: Politiques publiques et corporatismes*. Paris, France: Presses Universitaires de France.

Jourdan, A. (2004). *Mythes et légendes de Napoléon: Un destin d'exception entre rêve et réalité*. Toulouse, France: Privat.

Kapralski, S. (2012). Symbols and rituals in the mobilization of the Eomani national ideal. *Studies in ethnicity and nationalism, 12*(1), pp. 64–81.

Kaufman, J. (2004). Endogenous explanation in the sociology of culture. *Annual Review of Sociology, 30*, pp. 335–357.

Kirk, G. S. (1970). *Myth: Its meaning and functions in ancient and other cultures*. Berkeley, CA: University of California Press.

Kirschke, A. H. (2007). *Art in crisis: W. E. B. Du Bois and the struggle for African American identity and memory*. Bloomington, IN: Indiana University Press.

Kolakowski, L. (1989). *The presence of myth*. Chicago, IL: University of Chicago Press.

Kolakowski, L. (2008). *Main currents of Marxism: The founders, the golden age, the breakdown*. New York, NY: W. W. Norton.

Kramer, L. (2011). *Nationalism in Europe and America: Politics, culture, and identities since 1775*. Chapel Hill, NC: University of North Carolina Press.

Kuhn, T. (1962). *The structure of scientific revolutions*. Chicago, IL: University of Chicago Press.

Kumar, K. (2013). 1066 and all that: Myths of the English. In G. Bouchard (Ed.), *National myths: Constructed pasts, contested presents* (pp. 94–109). London, UK: Routledge.

Kymlicka, W. (2013). Neo-liberal multiculturalism? In P. Hall & M. Lamont (Eds.), *Resilience and neo-liberalism* (pp. 99–125). Cambridge, UK: Cambridge University Press.

Laclau, E., & Mouffe, C. (1985). *Hegemony and socialist strategy: Towards a radical democratic politics*. London, UK: Verso.

Lacroix, B. (1982). Imaginaire, merveilleux et sacré avec J.-C. Falardeau. In F. Dumont & Y. Martin (Eds.), *Imaginaire social et représentations collectives* (pp. 109–124). Québec, QC: Presses de l'Université Laval.

Lahire, B., & Rosental, C. (Eds.) (2008). *La Cognition au prisme des sciences sociales*. Paris, France: Éditions des Archives contemporaines.

Lakoff, G., Dean, H., & Hazen, D. (2004). *Don't think of an elephant! Know your values and frame the debate: The essential guide for the progressives*. White River Junction, VT: Chelsea Green.

Lamont, M. (2000). The rhetoric of racism and anti-racism in France and the United States. In M. Lamont & L. Thévenot (Eds.), *Rethinking comparative cultural sociology: Repertoires of evaluation in France and the United States* (pp. 25–55). London: Cambridge University Press; Paris, France: Maison des sciences de l'homme.

Lamont, M. (2002). *La Dignité des travailleurs: Exclusion, race, classe, et immigration en France et aux États-Unis*. Paris, France: Presses de Sciences Po.

Lamont, M., & Small, M. L. (2008). How culture matters: Enriching our understanding of poverty. In A. C. Lin & D. R. Harris (Eds.), *The Colors of Poverty: Why Racial and Ethnic Disparities Persist*. New York, NY: Russell Sage Foundation.

Lamont, M., & Thévenot, L. (2000). Introduction: Toward a renewed comparative cultural sociology. In M. Lamont & L. Thévenot (Eds.), *Rethinking comparative cultural sociology: Repertoires of evaluation in France and the United States* (pp. 1–22). London: Cambridge University Press; Paris, France: Maison des sciences de l'homme.

Laplanche, J., & Pontalis, J.-B. (1988). *Vocabulaire de la psychanalyse*. Paris, France: Presses Universitaires de France.

Laplantine, F. (1974). *Les Trois Voies de l'imaginaire*. Paris, France: Éditions universitaires.

Laroche, M. (1970). *Le Miracle et la métamorphose: Essai sur les littératures du Québec et d'Haïti*. Montrál, QC: Éditions du Jour.

Lasso, M. (2007). *Myths of harmony: Race and Republicanism during the age of revolution, Colombia, 1795–1831*. Pittsburgh, PA: University of Pittsburgh Press.

Latimer, J. (2007). *1812: War with America*. Cambridge, MA: Belknap Press of Harvard University Press.

Latour, B. (1988). *Science in action: How to follow scientists and engineers through society*. Cambridge, MA: Harvard University Press.

Leonard, S., & McClure, M. (2004). *Myth and knowing: An introduction to world mythology*. Boston, MA: McGraw-Hill.

Le Quellec, J.-L. (2013). *Jung et les archétypes: Un mythe contemporain*. Paris, France: Sciences humaines.

Levinger, M., & Franklin Lytle, P. (2001). Myth and mobilisation: The triadic structure of nationalist rhetoric. *Nations and Nationalism*, 7(2), pp. 175–194.

Lévi-Strauss, C. (1963). *Structural anthropology*. Trans. C. Jacobson and B. Grundfest Schoepf. New York, NY: Basic Books.

Lévi-Strauss, C. (1966). *The savage mind*. Trans. J. Weightman & D. Weightman. Chicago, IL: University of Chicago Press.

Lévi-Strauss, C. (1969–81). *Mythologiques I–IV*. Trans. J. Weightman & D. Weightman. Chicago, IL: University of Chicago Press.

Levitt, P., & Merry, S. (2009). Vernacularization on the ground: Local uses of global women's rights in Peru, China, India, and the United States. *Global Networks*, 9(4), pp. 441–461.

Lincoln, B. (1992). *Discourse and the construction of society: Comparative studies of myths*. Oxford, UK: Oxford University Press.

Lincoln, B. (2000). *Theorizing myth: Narrative, ideology, and scholarship*. Chicago, IL: University of Chicago Press.

Löfgren, O. (1989). The nationalization of culture. *Ethnologia Europaea*, 19(1), pp. 5–24.

Lukacs, G. (1989). *Théorie du roman*. Paris, France: Gallimard.

Lupasco, S. (1982). *Les Trois Matières*. Strasbourg, France: Cohérence.

Lupasco, S. (1987). *Le Principe d'antagonisme et la logique de l'énergie: Prolégomènes à une science des contradictions*. Monaco: Éditions du Rocher.

Luse, A., & Lazar, I. (Eds.) (2007). *Cosmologies of suffering: Post-communist transformation, sacral communication, and healing*. Newcastle upon Tyne, UK: Cambridge Scholars Publishing.

Maalouf, A. (2000). *In the name of identity: Violence and the need to belong*. Trans. Barbara Bray. New York, NY: Arcade.

Maffesoli, M. (2005). *Éloge de la raison sensible*. Paris, France: Table ronde.

Mann, T. (2005). *Joseph and his brothers*. Trans. J. E. Woods. New York: Alfred A. Knopf.

March, J. G., & Olsen, J. P. (1975). The uncertainty of the past: Organizational learning under ambiguity. *European Journal of Political Research*, 3, pp. 147–171.

Marx, L. (1964). *The machine in the garden: Technology and the pastoral ideal in America*. New York, NY: Oxford University Press.

Massenzio, M. (2002). *Claude Lévi-Strauss, un itinéraire: Entretien avec Marcello Massenzio*. Paris, France: L'Échoppe.

Matsuda, M. K. (2003). Idols of the emperor. In J. K. Olick (Ed.), *States of memory: Continuities, conflicts, and transformations in national retrospection* (pp. 72–100). Durham, NC: Duke University Press.

McAdam, D., McCarthy, J. D., & Zald, M. N. (Eds.). (1996). *Comparative perspectives on social movements: Political opportunities, mobilizing structures, and cultural framings*. Cambridge, MA: Cambridge University Press.

McDonald, L. C. (1969). Myths, politics, and political science. *Western Political Quarterly, 22*(1), pp. 141–150.

Melançon, B. (2006). *Les Yeux de Maurice Richard: Une histoire culturelle.* Montréal, QC: Fides.

Meney, L. (2010). *Main basse sur la langue: Idéologie et interventionnisme linguistique au Québec.* Montréal, QC: Liber.

Meyer, J. W., & Rowan, B. (1977). Institutionalized organizations: Formal structure as myth and ceremony. *American Journal of Sociology, 83*(2), pp. 340–363.

Mihelj, S. (2007). Faith in nations comes in different guises: Modernist versions of religious nationalism. *Nations and Nationalism, 13*(2), pp. 265–284.

Mishra, P. (2012). *From the ruins of empire: The intellectuals who remade Asia.* New York, NY: Farrar, Straus and Giroux.

Mock, S. J. (2012a). *Symbols of defeat in the construction of national identity.* New York, NY: Cambridge University Press.

Mock, S. J. (2012b). Whose game they're playing: Nation and emotion in Canadian TV advertising during the 2010 Winter Olympics. *Studies in Ethnicity and Nationalism, 12*(1), pp. 206–226.

Molnár, V. (2005). Cultural politics and modernist architecture: The tulip debate in postwar Hungary. *American Sociological Review, 70,* pp. 111–135.

Moscovici, S. (1984). The phenomenon of social representations. In R. M. Farr & S. Moscovici (Eds.), *Social representations* (pp. 3–69). Cambridge, UK: Cambridge University Press; Paris, France: Éditions de la maison des sciences de l'homme.

Nardout-Lafarge, É. (2001). *La Poétique du débris.* Montrál, QC: Fides.

Nareau, M. (2007). Le mythe états-unien du baseball. In G. Bouchard & B. Andrès (Eds.), *Mythes et sociétés des Amériques* (pp. 173–204). Montréal, QC: Québec Amérique.

Nelles, H. V. (2003). *L'Histoire spectacle: Le cas du tricentenaire de Québec.* Montréal, QC: Boréal.

O'Connor, J. S., & Olsen, G. M. (Eds.) (1998). *Power resource theory and the welfare state: A critical approach.* Toronto, ON: University of Toronto Press.

Olick, J. K. (1999). Collective memory: The two cultures. *Sociological Theory, 17*(3), pp. 333–348.

Olson, L. C. (2004). *Benjamin Franklin's vision of American community: A study in rhetorical iconology.* Columbia, SC: University of South Carolina Press.

Ombrosi, O. (2007). *Le Crépuscule de la raison: Benjamin, Adorno, Horkheimer, et Lévinas à l'épreuve de la Catastrophe.* Paris, France: Hermann.

Otto, R. (1968). *Le Sacré.* Paris, France: Payot.

Otto, W. F. (1987). *Essais sur le mythe.* Mauvezin, France: Trans-Europ-Repress.

Paces, C. (2009). *Prague panoramas: National memory and sacred space in the twentieth century*. Pittsburgh, PA: University of Pittsburgh Press.

Parent, A.-M. (2006). Trauma, témoignage, et récit: la déroute du sens. *Protée*, *34*(2–3), pp. 113–125.

Passerini, L. (2003). Dimension of the symbolic in the construction of Europeanness. In L. Passerini, *Figures d'Europe: Images and myths of Europe* (pp. 21–33). Brussels, Belgium: P.-I.-E. Lang.

Pelletier, J. (1991). *Le Roman national*. Montréal, QC: VLB.

Perrier-Bruslé, L. (2011). Le retour de la revendication maritime bolivienne. *Ceriscope Frontières*. http://ceriscope.sciences-po.fr/node/192.

Perrier-Bruslé, L. (2013). La Bolivie, sa mer perdue et la construction nationale. *Annales de géographie*, *1*(689), pp. 47–72.

Perrot, M.-D., Rist, G., & Sabelli, F. (1992). *La Mythologie programmée: L'économie des croyances dans la société moderne*. Paris, France: Presses Universitaires de France.

Pessin, A. (2001). *L'Imaginaire utopique aujourd'hui*. Paris, France: Presses Universitaires de France.

Peterson, R. A. (2000). Two ways culture is produced. *Poetics*, *28*(2–3), pp. 225–233.

Petersen, R. D. (2011). *Western intervention in the Balkans: The strategic use of emotion in conflict*. Cambridge, UK: Cambridge University Press.

Pettazzoni, R. (1984). The truth of myths. In A. Dundes (Ed.), *Sacred narrative: Reading in the theory of myth* (pp. 98–109). Berkeley, CA: University of California Press.

Pizzorno, A. (1986). Some other kinds of otherness: A critique of "rational choice" theories. In A. Foxley, M. McPherson, & G. O'Donnell (Eds.), *Development democracy and the art of trespassing: Essays in honor of Albert O. Hirschman* (pp. 355–372). Notre Dame, IN: University of Notre Dame Press.

Polletta, F. (2006). *It was like a fever: Storytelling in protests and politics*. Chicago, IL: University of Chicago Press.

Polletta, F., & Ho, M. K. (2006). Frames and their consequences. In R. E. Goodin & C. Tilly (Eds.), *The Oxford handbook of contextual political analysis* (pp. 187–209). Oxford, UK: Oxford University Press.

Polletta, F., Chen, P. C. B., Gardner, B. G., & Motes, A. (2011). The sociology of storytelling. *Annual Review of Sociology*, *37*, pp. 109–130.

Popper. K. R. (2002). *Conjectures and refutations: The growth of scientific knowledge*. New York, NY: Harper and Row.

Prokop, J. (1995). Mythes fondateurs staliniens en Pologne après 1945. Continuités et ruptures. *Iris*, *15* ("Mythes et Nation"), pp. 157–169.

Raffard, M.-H. (2013). Le décor mythique dans l'oeuvre de Michel Tremblay. In R. Laprée and C.-R. Belhumeur (Eds.), *L'Imaginaire durandien: Enracinements et envol en terre d'Amérique* (pp. 225–244). Québec, QC: Presses de l'Université Laval.

Raffestin, C., & Bresso, M. (1982). Tradition, modernité, territorialité. *Cahiers de géographie du Québec, 26*(68), pp. 186–198.

Ray, B. C. (1993). Victor Turner. In M. Eliade (Ed.), *Encyclopedia of religion*. New York, NY: Macmillan.

Reddy, W. M. (2001). *The navigation of feeling: A framework for the history of emotions*. Cambridge, UK: Cambridge University Press.

Reynaud-Paligot, C. (2006). *La République raciale: Paradigme racial et idéologie républicaine (1860–1930)*. Paris, France: Presses Universitaires de France.

Riall, L. (2007). *Garibaldi: Invention of a hero*. New Haven, CT: Yale University Press.

Rodgers, D. T. (1998). *Atlantic crossings: Social politics in a progressive age*. Cambridge, MA: Harvard University Press.

Roeder, P. G. (2007). *Where nation-states come from: Institutional change in the age of nationalism*. Princeton, NJ: Princeton University Press.

Rosental, C. (2003). Certifying knowledge: The sociology of a logical theorem in artificial intelligence. *American Sociological Review, 68*(4), pp. 623–644.

Roshwald, A. (2006). *The endurance of nationalism: Ancient roots and modern dilemmas*. Cambridge, UK: Cambridge University Press.

Rothberg, M. (2009) *Multidirectional memory: Remembering the Holocaust in the age of decolonization*. Stanford, CA: Stanford University Press.

Rudin, R. (2005). *L'Histoire dans les rues de Québec: La célébration de Champlain et de Mgr de Laval*. Québec, QC: Presses de l'Université Laval.

Rudin, R. (2009). *Remembering and forgetting in Acadie: A historian's journey through public memory*. Toronto, ON: University of Toronto Press.

Schell, O., & Delury, J. (2013). *Wealth and power: China's long march to the twenty-first century*. New York, NY: Random House.

Schilbrack, K. (2002). *Thinking through myths: Philosophical perspectives*. London, UK, and New York, NY: Routledge.

Schnapper, D. (1994). *La Communauté des citoyens: Sur l'idée moderne de nation*. Paris, France: Gallimard.

Schöpflin, G. (1997). The functions of myths and a taxonomy of myths. In G. Hosking & G. Schöpflin (Eds.), *Myths and nationhood* (pp. 19–35). New York, NY: Routledge.

Schudson, M. (1989). How culture works: Perspectives from media studies on the efficacy of symbols. *Theory and Society, 18*, pp. 153–180.

Schwartz, B., & Kim, M. (2002). Honor, dignity, and collective memory: Judging the past in Korea and the United States. In K. A. Cerulo (Ed.), *Culture in mind: Toward a sociology of culture and cognition* (pp. 209–226). New York, NY: Routledge.

Sciortino, G. (2012). Ethnicity, race, nationhood, foreignness, and many other things: Prolegomena to a cultural sociology of difference-based interactions. In J. C. Alexander, R. N. Jacobs, & P. Smith (Eds.), *The Oxford handbook of cultural sociology* (pp. 365–389). New York, NY: Oxford University Press.

Seelye, J. (1998). *Memory's nation: The place of Plymouth Rock.* Chapel Hill, NC: University of North Carolina Press.

Segal, R. A. (1999). *Theorizing about myths.* Amherst, MA: University of Massachusetts Press.

Seidman, S. (2011). The politics of authenticity: Civic individualism and the cultural roots of gay normalization. *Cultural Sociology, 5*(4), pp. 519–536.

Sellier, P. (1984). Qu'est-ce qu'un mythe littéraire? *Littérature, 55,* pp. 112–126.

Sewell, W. H. (1999). The concept(s) of culture. In V. E. Bonnell & L. Hunt (Eds.), *Beyond the cultural turn: New directions in the study of society and culture* (pp. 35–61). Berkeley, CA: University of California Press.

Shils, E. A. (1975). *Center and periphery: Essays in macrosociology.* Chicago, IL: University of Chicago Press.

Shore, B. (1998). *Culture in mind: Cognition, culture, and the problem of meaning.* New York, NY: Oxford University Press.

Sironneau, J.-P. (1995). Mythe et nation dans l'Allemagne moderne: De l'ethnie à l'idéologie. *Iris, 15* (Mythes et nation), pp. 41–62.

Slotkin, R. (1973). *Regeneration through violence: The mythology of the American frontier, 1600–1860.* Middletown, CT: Wesleyan University Press.

Slotkin, R. (1986). Myth and the production of history. In S. Bercovitch & M. Jehlen (Eds.), *Ideology and classic American literature* (pp. 70–90). Cambridge, UK: Cambridge University Press.

Smelser, N. J. (1962). *Theory of collective behavior.* London, UK: Routledge and Kegan Paul.

Smelser, N. J. (2004) Psychological trauma and cultural trauma. In J. C. Alexander, R. Eyerman, B. Giesen, N. J. Smelser, & P. Sztompka. *Cultural trauma and collective identity* (pp. 31–59). Berkeley, CA: University of California Press.

Smith, A. D. (1986). *The ethnic origins of nations.* Oxford, UK: Basil Blackwell.

Smith, P. (2012). Narrating global warming. In J. C. Alexander and P. Smith (Eds.), *The handbook of cultural sociology* (pp. 745–760). New York, NY: Oxford University Press.

Snow, D. A., Rochford, E. B., Worden, S. K., & Benford, R. D. (1986). Frame alignment processes, micromobilization, and movement participation. *American Sociological Review, 51*(4), pp. 464–481.

Snow, D. A., & Benford, R. D. (1988). Ideology, frame resonance, and participant mobilization. *International Social Movement Research, 1*, pp. 197–219.

Snow, D. A., & Benford, R. D. (1992). Master frames and cycles of protest. In A. D. Morris and C. M. Mueller, *Frontiers in social movement theory* (pp. 133–155). New Haven, CT: Yale University Press.

Snow, D. A., Soule, S. A., & Kriesi, H. (Eds.). (2004). *The Blackwell companion to social movements*. Oxford, UK: Wiley-Blackwell.

Soboul, A. (1983). Religious feeling and popular cults during the French Revolution: "Patriot Saints" and Martyrs of Liberty. In S. Wilson, *Saints and their cults: Studies in religious sociology, folklore, and history* (pp. 217–230). Cambridge, UK: Cambridge University Press.

Somers, M. R., & Block, F. (2005). From poverty to perversity: Ideas, markets, and institutions over 200 years of welfare debate. *American Sociological Review, 70*(2), pp. 260–287.

Sorel, G. (1999). *Reflections on violence*. Trans. J. L. Stanley. Cambridge, UK: Cambridge University Press.

Sorokin, P. (1970). *Social and cultural dynamics*. Boston, MA: Porter Sargent.

Spillman, L. (1997). *Nation and commemoration: Creating national identities in the United States and Australia*. Cambridge, UK: Cambridge University Press.

Spillman, L. (Ed.). (2002). *Cultural sociology*. Malden, MA: Blackwell.

Spillman, L. (2003). When do collective memories last? Founding moments in the United States and Australia. In J. K. Olick (Ed.), *States of memory: Continuities, conflicts, and transformations in national retrospection* (pp. 161–192). Durham, NC: Duke University Press.

Spiro, M. E. (1966). Buddhism and economic action in Burma. *American Anthropologist, 68*(5), pp. 1163–1173.

Spiro, M. E. (1987). Collective representations and mental representations in religious systems. In B. Kilborn & L. Langness (Eds.), *Culture and human nature: Theoretical papers of Melford E. Spiro* (pp. 161–184). Chicago, IL: University of Chicago Press.

Starobinski, J. (2001). *L'Oeil vivant, tome 2: La Relation critique*. Paris, France: Gallimard.

Steblin Kamenskij, M. I., & Liberman, A. (1982). *Myth: The Icelandic sagas and eddas*. Ann Arbor, MI: Karoma.

Strang, D., & Soule, S. A. (1998). Diffusion in organizations and social movements: From hybrid corn to poison pills. *Annual Review of Sociology, 24*, pp. 265–290.

Swidler, A. (1986). Culture in Action: Symbols and Strategies. *American Sociological Review*, 51(2), pp. 273–286.

Swidler, A. (2002). Saving the self: Endowment vs depletion in American institutions. In R. Madsen et al. (Eds.), *Meaning and modernity: Religion, polity, and self* (pp. 41–55). Berkeley, CA: University of California Press.

Sztompka, P. (2000). Cultural trauma: The other face of social change. *European Journal of Social Theory*, 3(4), pp. 449–466.

Taylor, C. (2002). Modern social imaginaries. *Public Culture*, 14(1), pp. 91–124.

Thériault, J.-Y. (2013). *Évangéline: Contes d'Amérique*. Montréal, QC: Québec Amérique.

Thibeault, J. (2015), *Des identités mouvantes: Se définir dans le contexte de la mondialisation*. Montréal, QC: Nota Bene.

Thiesse, A.-M. (1997). *Ils apprenaient la France: L'exaltation des régions dans le discours patriotique*. Paris, France: Éditions de la Maison des sciences de l'homme.

Thomas, J. (Ed.). (1998). *Introduction aux méthodologies de l'imaginaire*. Paris, France: Ellipses.

Thompson, K. (2012). Globalization and religion. In J. C. Alexander, R. N. Jacobs, & P. Smith (Eds.), *The Oxford handbook of cultural sociology* (chapter 17, pp. 471–483). New York, NY: Oxford University Press.

Tilly, C. (1995). Contentious repertoires in Great Britain, 1758–1834. In M. Traugott (Ed.), *Repertoires and cycles of collective action* (pp. 15–42). Durham, NC: Duke University Press.

Tilly, C. (2006). *Regimes and repertoires*. Chicago, IL: University of Chicago Press.

Toulmin, S. (1990). *Cosmopolis: The hidden agenda of modernity*. New York, NY: Free Press.

Touraine, A. (1965). *Sociologie de l'action*. Paris, France: Seuil.

Traugott, M. (Ed.). (1995). *Repertoires and cycles of collective action*. Durham, NC: Duke University Press.

Trice, H. M., & Beyer, J. M. (1984). Studying organizational cultures through rites and ceremonials. *Academy of Management Review*, 9(4), pp. 653–669.

Trousson, P. (1995). *Le Recours de la science au mythe: Pour une nouvelle rationalité*. Paris, France: L'Harmattan.

Tsai, L. L. (2007). *Solidarity groups and public goods provision in rural China*. Cambridge, MA: Cambridge University Press.

Tudor, H. (1972). *Political myth*. New York, NY: Praeger Publishers.

Tully, S. (2005). An analysis of "myth and symbol." *Chronicle of Higher Education*, 51(53), pp. 1–3.

Türkmen-Dervisoglu, G. (2013). Coming to terms with a difficult past: The trauma of the assassination of Hrant Dink and its repercussions on Turkish national identity. *Nations and Nationalism, 19*(4), pp. 674–692.

Tyrrell, I. (2013). The myth that will not die. In G. Bouchard (Ed.), *National myths: Constructed pasts, contested presents* (pp. 46–64). London, UK: Routledge.

Utéza, F. (2007). Mythe et littérature: Héros blanc et ombres noires dans le *Romanceiro da Inconfidência*. In G. Bouchard & B. Andrès (Eds.), *Mythes et sociétés des Amériques* (pp. 49–87). Montréal, QC: Québec Amérique.

Vacher, L.-M. (2002). *Débats philosophiques: Une initiation*. Montréal, QC: Liber.

Vadeboncoeur, P. (2002). L'équation à mille inconnues. *L'Inconvénient, 11*, pp. 67–69.

Vernant, J.-P. (1974). *Mythe et société en Grèce ancienne*. Paris, France: François Maspéro.

Veyne, P. (1983). *Les Grecs ont-ils cru à leurs mythes? Essai sur l'imagination constituante*. Paris, France: Seuil.

Vlastos, S. (2013). Lineages and lessons (for national myth formation) of Japan's postwar national myths. In G. Bouchard (Ed.), *National myths: Constructed pasts, contested presents* (pp. 243–258). London: Routledge.

Von Hendy, A. (2002). *The modern construction of myth*. Bloomington, IN: Indiana University Press.

Wagner-Pacifici, R., & Schwartz, B. (2002). The Vietnam Veterans Memorial: Commemorating a difficult past. In L. Spillman (Ed.), *Cultural sociology* (pp. 210–220). Malden, MA: Blackwell Publishers.

Wang, Z. (2012). *Never forget national humiliation: Historical memory in Chinese politics and foreign relations*. New York, NY: Columbia University Press.

Weisinger, H. (1964). *The agony and the triumph: Papers on the use and abuse of myth*. Ann Arbor, MI: University of Michigan Press.

Wheelwright, P. (1955). The semantic approach to myth. *Journal of American Folklore, 68*(270), pp. 473–481.

White, H. (1999). *Figural realism: Studies in the Mimesis Effect*. Baltimore, MD: Johns Hopkins University Press.

White, R., Limerick, P. N., & Grossman, J. R. (1994). *The frontier in American culture*. Berkeley, CA: University of California Press.

Wieviorka, O. (2012). *Divided memory: French recollections of World War II from the liberation to the present*. Stanford, CA: Stanford University Press.

Wilson, A. (1997). Myths of national history in Belarus and Ukraine. In G. Hosking & G. Schöpflin (Eds.), *Myths and nationhood* (pp. 182–197). New York, NY: Routledge.

Woolf, V. (1925). *The common reader*. London, UK: Penguin.

Wunenburger, J.-J. (1995). *L'Imagination*. Paris, France: Presses Universitaires de France.

Wunenburger, J.-J. (2001). *Imaginaires du politique*. Paris, France: Ellipses.

Wunenburger, J.-J. (2006). *L'Imaginaire*. Paris, France: Presses Universitaires de France.

Wunenburger, J.-J. (2009). *Le Sacré*. Paris, France: Presses Universitaires de France.

Wuthnow, R. (1989). *Communities of discourse: Ideology and social structure in the Reformation, the Enlightenment, and European socialism*. Cambridge, MA: Harvard University Press.

Zerubavel, Y. (1995). *Recovered roots: Collective memory and the making of Israeli national tradition*. Chicago, IL: University of Chicago Press.

Zerubavel, Y. (2013). Transforming myths, contested narratives: The reshaping of mnemonic traditions in Israeli culture. In G. Bouchard (Ed.), *National myths: Constructed pasts, contested presents* (pp. 173–190). London, UK: Routledge.

Zubrzycki, G. (2013a). History, the national sensorium, and the traps of Polish messianic martyrology. In G. Bouchard (Ed.), *National myths: Constructed pasts, contested presents* (pp. 110–132). London, UK: Routledge.

Zubrzycki, G. (2013b). Aesthetic revolt and the remaking of national identity in Quebec, 1960–1969. *Theory and Society, 42*(5), pp. 423–475.

Index

www.ingramcontent.com/pod-product-compliance
Ingram Content Group UK Ltd.
Pitfield, Milton Keynes, MK11 3LW, UK
UKHW032122310125
454513UK00004B/158